REALLY
Jazzy Jars

CHICKEN NOODLE SOUP

- 1 jar Chicken Noodle Soup Mix
- 8 cups water
- 2 carrots, diced
- 2 stalks celery, diced
- ¼ cup minced onion
- 3 cup cooked chicken

Simmer all ingredients except the meat for about 15 minutes. Add the meat in last 5 minutes of cooking.

R E A L L Y
Jazzy Jars
GLORIOUS GIFT IDEAS

Marie Browning

Sterling Publishing Co., Inc.
New York

Prolific Impressions Production Staff:

Editor in Chief: Mickey Baskett
Copy Editor: Phyllis Mueller
Graphics: Dianne Miller, Karen Turpin
Styling: Lenos Key Jones
Photography: Jerry Mucklow
Administration: Jim Baskett

Library of Congress Cataloging-in-Publication Data Available
Browning, Marie.
  Really jazzy jars : glorious gift ideas / Marie Browning.
      p. cm.
  Includes index.
  ISBN 1-4027-1473-4
  1. Handicraft. 2. Storage jars. 3. Decoration and ornament. I. Title.
  TT157.B787 2005
  745.5--dc22

                                                  2004018172

10 9 8 7 6 5 4 3 2 1

Published by Sterling Publishing Co., Inc.
387 Park Avenue South, New York, N.Y. 10016

© 2005 by Prolific Impressions, Inc.
Produced by Prolific Impressions, Inc.
160 South Candler St., Decatur, GA 30030

Distributed in Canada by Sterling Publishing
c/o Manda Group, 165 Dufferin Street
Toronto , Ontario, Canada M6K 3H6
Distributed in Great Britain by Chrysalis Books Group PLC,
The Chrysalis Building, Bramley Road, London W10 6SP, England
Distributed in Australia by Capricorn Link (Australia) Pty. Ltd.
P.O. Box 704, Windsor, NSW 2756 Australia

Printed in China
All rights reserved
Sterling ISBN 1-4027-1473-4

Acknowledgments

I thank these companies for their generous contributions of quality products and support in the creation of the projects in this book:

For glass jars, canning jars, antique jar reproductions: Alltrista Corporation, Indianapolis, IN 46250, www.alltrista.com

For colored wire: Artistic Wire, 1210 Harrison Ave., LaGrange Park, IL, www.artisticwire.com

For metal charms: Boutique Trims, South Lyon, MI 48178, www. boutiquetrims.com

For opaque and transparent PermEnamel paints for glass and for stencils: Delta Technical Coatings, Inc., Whittier, CA 90601, www.deltacrafts.com

For Envirotex Lite (two part resin coating), AromaGel, (waterbase gel air freshener), colorants, fragrances, jars, and perforated lids: Environmental Technologies, Fields Landing, CA 95537, www.eti-usa.com

For vintage peel-and-stick labels and jar lamp kits: Heart & Home Collectibles Inc., Ajax, Ontario, Canada L1S 6W3, www.melissafrances.com

For Painters opaque paint markers: Hunt Corporation, 2005 Market St., Philadelphia, PA 19103, www.hunt-corp.com

For spray paints: Krylon, 101 Prospect Ave., NW, Cleveland, OH 44115, www.krylon.com

For acrylic high gloss enamel paint for glass, Royal Coat® Decoupage Finish, FolkArt® Papier dimensional fabric paints, and Stencil Decor® stencils: Plaid Enterprises, Norcross, GA 30091, www.plaidonline.com

For Sculpey and Premo brands of polymer clay and polymer clay tools: Polyform Products, 1901 Estes Ave., Elk Grove Village, IL, www.sculpey.com

ABOUT THE AUTHOR
Marie Browning

Marie Browning is a consummate craft designer who has made a career of designing products, writing books and articles, and teaching and demonstrating. You may have been charmed by her creative acumen but not been aware of the woman behind it; she has designed stencils, stamps, transfers, and a variety of other award winning product lines for art and craft supply companies.

She is the author of five books on soapmaking: *Beautiful Handmade Natural Soaps* (Sterling, 1998), *Melt & Pour Soapmaking* (Sterling, 2000), *300 Handcrafted Soaps* (Sterling, 2002) *Designer Soapmaking* (Sterling 2003) and *Totally Cool Soapmaking for Kids* (Sterling, 2004). In addition to books about soapmaking, Browning has authored eight other books published by Sterling; *Handcrafted journals, Albums, Scrapbooks & More* (1999), *Making Glorious Gifts from your Garden* (1999), *Memory Gifts* (2000), *Hand Decorating Paper* (2000), *Crafting with Vellum and Parchment* (2001), *Jazzy Jars* (2003) and *Wonderful Wraps* (2003), and *Really Jazzy Jars* (2005). Her articles and designs have appeared numerous home dÈcor and crafts magazines and in numerous project books published by Plaid Enterprises, Inc.

Marie Browning earned a Fine Arts Diploma from Camosun College and attended the University of Victoria. She is a Certified Professional Demonstrator, a design member of the Crafts and Hobby Association and a member of the Society of Craft Designers (SCD). Marie also is on the trend committee for SCD that researches and writes about upcoming trends in the arts and crafts industry. In 2004 Marie was selected by Craftrends trade publication as a "Top Influential Industry Designer".

She lives, gardens and crafts on Vancouver Island in Canada. She and her husband Scott have three children: Katelyn, Lena and Jonathan. Marie can be contacted at www.mariebrowning.com. ❏

CONTENTS

More than
75
Decorated
Jar Projects

DECORATING JARS and filling them with homemade treats is rewarding for the giver and delightful for the recipient because a decorated jar is a gift of your time, thoughts, and creativity. The jar creates a wonderful presentation, and it can become a decorative storage container after its contents are used up.

This book includes ideas and instructions for making more than 75 decorated jar projects that are suitable for both the novice and experienced crafters. There are simple but beautiful painting

projects, fun ideas for using polymer clay and plastic foam balls, memory jars, altered art jars, and fabulous ideas for gel air fresheners and food gifts in jars – a wealth of ideas.

Candle bases, storage jars, and gift jars are great ways to recycle jars and an economical way to create lots of gifts. Quart-size jars can be filled with layered mixes (some of my favorite recipes appear at the end of the book), cookies, or treats. Pint-size canning jars are perfect for banks, pencil holders, or desk storage jars. Apothecary jars can be decorated for bathroom use, and any size works as a vase for fresh flowers.

Gifts made with the hands and given from the heart are always appreciated and remembered fondly. Celebrate your originality with a special gift that expresses you as you experience the excitement of creating and the thrill of giving. Most of all, have fun!

A Brief History of Glass Jars

As far back in time as the ancient Egyptians, glass jars and bottles have been used as containers. The use of glass as a container for foods is, however, quite recent. The process of applying heat to kill bacteria and removing oxygen from jars to prevent food from deteriorating was invented in France in 1795 by Nicholas Appert. Appert, a chef, was determined to

win the prize of 12,000 francs offered by Napoleon for a way to prevent military food supplies from spoiling. The first process involved garden peas preserved in champagne bottles, and the French military secret soon was leaked to the English. By 1810 an Englishman, Peter Durance, had patented the use of metal containers for canning and was opening factories. By the 1860s, canned foods were commonplace.

The major companies that manufacture canning jars today – Ball, Mason, and Kerr – were all started at least 100 years ago. The Ball brothers, Frank and Edmund, founded the Ball Corporation in 1880. They started with a wood-jacketed tin container for paint and varnish and soon expanded into the home-canning field. Ball still produces glass canning jars as

well as space systems and electro-optic materials.

Jars used for home canning are often referred to as "Mason" jars after John L. Mason, inventor of the first common canning jar. Mason's patent expired in 1875. Since then, all canning jars are generally called mason jars. The first mason jars were made of blue-green glass. The originals are collectible and quite valuable.

The Kerr Company, founded in 1902, developed the two-piece lid, which is comprised of a flat seal and a separate screw-on band.

The inert, impermeable, transparent, and heat-resistant properties of glass makes it especially suitable for packaging and storing foods, and glass is the most popular vessel choice today. Glass jars usually are made by melting together sand, limestone, soda ash, and minor additives in a gas-fired furnace. The molten glass is then blown or molded into shapes. Glass jars are completely recyclable, inexpensive, and readily available.

Start with a Jar...

There are a variety of jar types you can use to decorate. Many of these types of jars listed can be recycled or purchased at grocery stores, craft stores, or container stores.

Mason-style Canning Jars: Mason jars are glass jars available in half-pint, pint, quart and half gallon sizes with a standard or wide opening, which is called the "mouth." The glass may be embossed with fruit motifs, diamond patterns, or company names and crests. Generally, plain jars were used for the projects in this book, but embossed jars can be substituted.

Old-fashioned Wire Bail Jars: These jars, which have a glass base and a glass lid that is held in place with a wire clamp, cost a little more but give the finished project a more sophisticated appearance. They are made in many sizes and shapes found at quality kitchen stores and department stores.

Apothecary Jars: These are great choices for elegant designs for the bathroom and bedroom. The glass jars generally have straight sides and are topped with a glass or metal lid.

Recycled Jars: Many jars can be recycled for gift giving. You can save jars all year and be ready with a nice selection whenever you wish to create a gift. Baby food jars, mayonnaise jars, and large spaghetti sauce jars are some of my favorites – and unlike canning jars, they have smooth sides. Soak the jars to remove the labels and wash them carefully to remove any food residue. Lids with printing can be covered with metal paints or fabric tops. Recycled jars are **not** recommended for canning foods.

Antique Jars: Antique glass jars are beautiful but more brittle than new jars and easier to break. Some are quite valuable; some early, colored canning jars have sold for $1,000 each! If you are not sure of the value of an old jar, it's wise not to use it. If you use one, make sure it is free of chips and imperfections. A good alternative is to use a reproduction antique jar.

Lids for Jars

Typical modern canning jar lids come in two parts, a flat metal lid and a screw-on band, called a "ring." Plastic screw-top lids are generally used for storage jars. Metal one-piece screw-top lids generally are used by food manufacturers; they can be reused when a seal is not required. Other types of jars have glass lids and wire clamps, wooden stoppers with rubber seals, and natural corks. You can buy perforated metal lids for fragrance gifts or make your own.

Jars are an excellent base for a candle or lamp – check out your local craft outlet for lamp fixtures that screw right on canning jars in place of the lid.

You can also find lid lamp kits for canning jars that allow you to use a decorated jar as an oil lamp. The screw-on lid has a hole; a glass vial fits into the lid and a stopper placed on the vial holds a wick. The glass vial can be filled with lamp oil.

Glass votive candle holders – especially the clear glass ones shaped like flower pots – fit nicely in the tops of quart-size canning jars that contain layered potpourri or other decorative items.

For safety's sake, always give instructions for the use of your lighted jar gift and remind the recipient to never leave a burning candle unattended.

Caring for Jars

Unless you are using acrylic enamel paint that can be baked or cured for permanency, most products you use on the jars are not permanent and are to be used on jars that are for decorative purposes only. Here are some tips and recommendations for keeping your decorated jars in good condition:

• For lasting color, spray a finished jar with a sealer. Choose from matte, satin, and gloss finishes, depending on the look you want.

• To clean a decorated jar, simply wipe with a soft, damp cloth.

• Jars coated with resin are much more durable and can withstand more moisture, for example, as use as a vase for outside.

• **Do not** immerse decorated jars in hot water, and do not leave decorated jars standing in water.

• **Do not** expose jars to extreme hot or cold temperatures.

• Remember that glass is fragile. Handle with care.

Supplies
&
Techniques

A variety of techniques can be used to decorate jars. For many techniques, all that's needed is the desire to decorate a blank canvas. This section explains the techniques I used for the projects throughout the book and the supplies you need to accomplish each technique.

PAINTING

STENCILING

DECOUPAGE

POLYMER CLAY

COATING WITH RESIN

CRACKLING

EMBELLISHING

DECOUPAGED JARS

With decoupage, you can decorate jars with many types of paper and fabric. You can choose to add a few cutout motifs, cover a jar completely, or compose a collage. Lightweight decoupage paper and gift wrapping paper are the best types of paper for decoupage. I also like to use printed napkins, handmade papers, and collage papers. You can also use fabrics to cover a jar – 100% cottons and cotton-polyester blends work best. Avoid using heavy fabrics like terrycloth and fabrics with a nap, such as velvet or corduroy. You will need two basic skills – careful cutting and gluing – to create heirloom quality projects you will be proud to display and give as gifts. Decoupage is done in three basic steps: cutting, gluing, and sealing. A "podge"-type decoupage medium can be used for both gluing and sealing. These types of jars can not be washed and are not meant for food storage. Use these for decorative purposes only.

Supplies for Decoupage

Paper or fabric of your choice for covering jar

Decoupage medium, sometimes labeled "decoupage finish"

Foam brush, for applying medium

Craft knife and **sharp scissors**, for cutting designs

Cutting mat, to use with a craft knife

Freezer paper, to cover your work surface

Optional:

Thin-bodied white glue, as an alternative for adhering paper or fabric

Waterbase varnish, for sealing

Two-part resin coating, for a waterproof finish

The Decoupage Technique

Cutting

Trim away excess paper from around the image, using a craft knife and cutting mat to remove any inside areas before cutting around the outer edges with small, sharp, pointed scissors. Hold the scissors at a 45-degree angle to create a tiny beveled edge on the paper. (This edge helps the image fit snugly against the surface.) Move the print, not the scissors as you cut.

Options: After cutting out an image, you can decorate it further with stamping or antique the edges with an ink pad and dense foam sponge.

Gluing

Cover your working surface with freezer paper to protect it. Use a 1" foam brush to lightly coat the back of the image with decoupage medium. (**photo 1**) Place in position on the surface and use your fingers to smooth it, pushing out wrinkles and air bubbles. (**photo 2**) Allow to dry before proceeding.

Sealing

To seal the decoupaged design, apply two to three coats of decoupage medium with the foam brush. The finish appears cloudy when wet but dries crystal clear. (**photo 3**)

If you are planning to coat your project with pour-on resin, seal the decoupaged surface with thin-bodied white glue.

PAINTED JARS

A nice variety of paints suitable for glass are available in a wide range of colors,
including opaque, transparent, and dimensional paints.
Transparent paint lines that give the glass the look of stained glass usually
include a liquid "leading" that can be used with the transparent colors. Acrylic
enamel paints suitable for glass also can be used on plastic jars.

Acrylic Enamel Paints

These types of paint are the most permanent and the ones you should use if the jar would ever need washing. Food can be stored inside of the jars when the painting is on the outside. Food should not come in contact with the paint.

These durable high-gloss acrylic paints for glass and ceramics offer a wide variety of pre-mixed colors. Follow the manufacturer's instructions for using and curing. Do not thin paints with water – use a medium manufactured for that brand of paint. While still wet, paints for glass clean up easily with soap and water.

When the paint has dried and cured (at least 48 hours), jars can be baked in a home oven for a very durable painted surface that is waterproof. After baking, painted jars can be washed. Follow the paint manufacturer's instructions for the brand you are using concerning curing and durability.

Transparent Paints

Acrylic transparent paints to look like stained glass are packaged in squeeze tubes for easy application and are available in a wide range of colors. Dimensional paint in gold, black, and silver are used to create simulated leading. You can also find simulated lead in ready-to-use strips with an adhesive backing. When these types of paints are used, the jars can not be washed.

Acrylic Paint for Metal

Use a paint especially manufactured for use on metal to paint the metal lids.

Dimensional Paint

Dimensional paints (sometimes called "fabric paints" or "dimensional paper paints") come in squeeze bottles with applicator tips. When completely dry and cured they are remarkably strong and durable. Dimensional paints are easy enough for children to use. These paints are not washable and should be used only on jars that are for decoration or will not need washing.

Paint Pens

Paint pens come in many colors and in fine, medium, and calligraphy chisel point tips. They're an easy way to add accents on jars or details on painted designs. If you're using them with other paints, be sure the paint is dry and fully cured before using a paint pen, and always test the pen to be sure it's compatible with the other paint. (TIP: Use the bottom of the jar.) Follow the manufacturer's directions for use.

Spray Paints

Spray paint is a wonderful way to create a smooth basecoat of color on a jar. It's also an easy way to paint the inside of a jar – just place the spray nozzle inside of the jar and spray. This close-up spraying will result in paint drips, but the drips won't show on the outside of the jar. Two coats are usually sufficient for full coverage. Be sure to aim the top of the jar away from your face while you spray the inside to avoid getting a face full of fumes, and **always** spray in a well-ventilated area. These paints are not meant to be used when placing food inside. They are not permanent and the jars can not be washed.

Texture Paint

Texture paint, which comes in tubs, is useful for adding texture. Although not recommended for glass, it can be used for lids. It dries hard and can be painted with acrylic craft paints. Apply texture paint with a plastic palette knife.

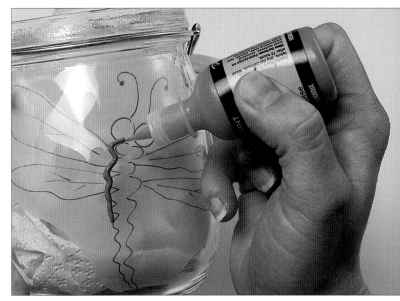

Dimensional paint is used here to outline the design.

Paint Applicators

You will need a variety of good quality artist's brushes for painting designs:
Flat brushes – 1/2" and 1", for basecoating and painting large motifs and #4, #6, and #10 for general painting and details
Round brushes – #1 and #4, for general painting and details
Liners – #1, #0, #00 for fine detailing

You'll also need some sponges:
Fine textured sea sponges, for basecoating and sponged finishes
Dense foam sponges – the type used for applying make-up, for stenciling

Other Basic Supplies for Painting

• Paper towels
• Water basin
• Low-tack ("painter's") masking tape
• Wax-free transfer paper and stylus
• Tracing paper and fine tip marker
• Palette or disposable foam plate or bowl
• Brush cleaner soap

Painting Techniques

Surface Preparation

Be sure the jar is clean and dry before applying paint. Rub the surface with rubbing alcohol or white vinegar, holding the jar by the jar neck to avoid fingerprints. Some glass paints require an undercoat. Follow the manufacturer's instructions for best results.

Transferring Designs

If the jar is transparent (not basecoated), you can trace the pattern and place it inside the jar, securing it at the top with a small piece of tape and placing two or three crumpled paper towels in the jar to hold the pattern against the glass. (This method is a lot easier than trying to place tape all around the pattern to hold it flat against the glass.)

When transferring a pattern to painted glass, use wax-free transfer paper. Carefully tape the transfer paper in place over the jar, making sure the paper is right side down, and tape the pattern on top. With a stylus or ballpoint pen, trace over the pattern lines firmly to transfer the design to the jar.

Placing a traced pattern inside a jar

Basecoating

Paints can be applied to jars in a number of ways for a full opaque coverage:

Brushing. Brush on the paint, using enough paint on your brush so the paint coats the glass without dripping. Two or three coats are usually needed. Let dry fully between coats.

Stippling: Apply the paint by pouncing with a sea sponge. Make sure the sponge is damp, not wet – squeeze out all the excess water. Pour a puddle of paint on a palette or disposable foam plate and dip the sponge in the paint to load. Pounce on the palette to distribute the paint through the sponge and apply to the jar in an up and down dabbing motion. You will need to apply two or three coats, letting each coat dry fully before applying the next. This method gives the finished surface a slight texture.

Spraying: Follow the manufacturer's instructions and work in a well-ventilated area. Avoid over-spraying when basecoating the outside of the jar as it will create unsightly drips.

Design Painting

Squeeze small puddles of the paint colors on a palette or disposable foam plate or bowl. Use the recommended brushes or other applicators to paint the design, following the step-by-step instructions in the individual project instructions.

Painting a design on a jar.

Stenciling

You can stencil designs on jars using a pre-cut purchased stencil or cut your own stencils from freezer paper.

1. To cut your own stencil, photocopy the pattern and tape the copy on a piece of freezer paper that is shiny side up and 1" larger all around than the pattern.

18

2. Place the papers on a cutting mat and cut out the motifs with a sharp craft knife.
3. Spray the backside of the stencil with a coat of spray adhesive. (This makes your stencil adhere to the jar and allows you to remove it without tearing.) (**photo 1**)
4. Let the adhesive dry for 10 minutes and position the stencil on the jar.
5. Squeeze a puddle of paint on a palette or disposable plate. Load a make-up sponge with paint by dabbing it in the puddle. (**photo 2**)
6. Press or dab the sponge on a paper towel to remove excess paint. (**photo 3**) The key here is to **use very little paint**. Glass is not forgiving; even a little too much paint can seep under the stencil, so it's better to use very little paint and apply as many coats as necessary to achieve the effect you want.
7. Stipple the color into the open areas of the stencil with an up and down dabbing motion. (**photo 4**) *Note:* The circular, swirling method of stenciling does not work on the slick glass surface.

Photo 1

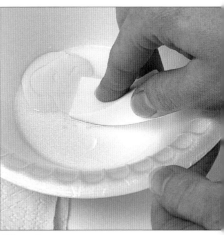

Photo 2

Photo 3

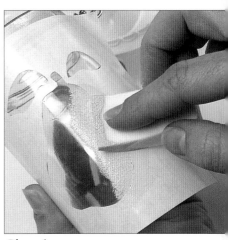

Photo 4

ANTIQUING & DISTRESSING

You can add the look of age and wear to your decorated jars with some simple paint techniques. You can use these techniques on painted, stenciled, and decoupaged designs.

Crackling

It's easy to get a fine crackled finish (sometimes called "eggshell crackle") with a crackle kit or with crackle medium. The kit (the one you want is usually labeled "varnish crackle," not "aged paint") typically includes a basecoat and a topcoat that both dry clear. (The varnishes dry at different rates, creating the fine crackles.) To make the cracks more visible, brush the surface with a contrasting acrylic craft paint color – white or light-hued paint over a dark image and dark brown or black paint over a light image – and immediately wipe off the excess to reveal the fine cracks.

If you use this product, you can not wash the jars. They are to be used for decoration only.

Continued on next page

Continued from page 19

Antiquing

An easy way to get an antique look on a surface painted with acrylic enamel paint is to use dark brown paint that has been thinned with the clear medium that is specifically for the paint. Brush the mixture over the surface, then wipe away any excess with a soft cloth rag.

To antique a surface that is not painted, use the appropriate paint for that surface. For example, thin glass paint with glass paint varnish or a clear medium and brush over the project.

COATING JARS & LIDS WITH RESIN

A two-part pour-on resin coating gives jars and lids a hard, waterproof finish with a depth and lustre equal to 50 coats of varnish. I use resin coating for many projects to give a professional look and a practical, easy-to-clean surface. The steps, under the decorative tops sections, are easy to follow and result in spectacular lids.

Basic Supplies for Resin Coating

Two-part pour-on resin coating

Mixing supplies: a plastic mixing cup with accurate measurement marks, a wooden stir stick, and a disposable glue brush (These items will be discarded after use.)

Freezer paper or wax paper, to protect your work surface

Disposable plastic or waxed paper cups, to prop up your project and keep it off the work surface

Thin-bodied white glue, for sealing

Clear cellophane tape or **rubber cement**, for masking surfaces

Fine sandpaper, for removing drips after drying

Applying the Coating

1. Protect the bottom of the jar with rubber cement or cellophane tape.

2. Seal all decorative treatments (paper and all porous materials) with a coat of thin-bodied white glue that dries clear. While it is drying, place the jar right side up on a waxed paper cup to lift it away from your work surface.

3. When the glue is dry, you are ready to mix the resin. The coating comes in two parts, the resin and the hardener. Mix only as much as you can use on your project – leftover coating cannot be saved for other projects. Measure out the two parts in the same container. You want to mix exactly 1 part resin with 1 part hardener. (**photo 1**)

4. Stir the resin and hardener with the wooden stick until thoroughly blended – this takes a full two minutes of vigorous mixing. The importance of thorough mixing cannot be over-emphasized, as poor mixing can result in a soft finish because the coating will not harden properly. Do not be concerned if bubbles get whipped into the mixture. Bubbles will be removed after the resin is poured.

5. As soon as the coating is mixed, pour it over the outside of your jar or lid. (**photo 2**) Allow the excess to drip off onto a protected surface.

6. Spread the coating, using a brush, as necessary. You have about 20 minutes to work on your project before the coating starts to set up.

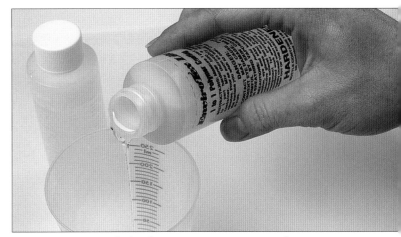
Photo 1 – Pouring the hardener into a measuring cup for mixing.

Photo 2 – Pouring the coating on a lid.

TIPS & CONSIDERATIONS

- Your work surface should be level and the area warm and free of dust.
- Your project surface should be dry and free of any dust or grease.
- The coating will drip off the sides of the project. You can protect the underside by brushing on rubber cement or lining the bottom edges with clear cellophane tape.
- Drips on unprotected surfaces can be sanded off when the finish has cured.

7. After 5 to 10 minutes, the air bubbles created when mixing will rise to the surface. They can be easily and effectively broken by gently exhaling on them until they disappear. (The carbon dioxide in your breath breaks the bubbles.) **Avoid inhaling fumes** as you de-gas the bubbles.

8. Discard the mixing cup, the stir stick, and the brush. Allow your project to cure for a full 72 hours to a hard, permanent finish. Remove the tape or rubber cement from the bottom of the jar. Sand off excess drips with fine sandpaper. ❑

POLYMER CLAY MOLDING

Polymer clay can be used to make three-dimensional accents for jars and lids. It's readily available, easy to work with, comes in a wide range of colors, and bakes in your home oven. You can mold it with your hands or with a purchased mold. The variety of molds available makes it even easier to create unique embellishments for jars. You can use sheets of polymer clay to cover jars and create designs in clay with tools or rubber stamps.
For best results, **always** follow the clay manufacturer's instructions carefully. Make sure you have sufficient ventilation during baking. After baked polymer clay has cooled, you can paint, varnish, sand, or drill it. Jars decorated with clay can not be washed.

Polymer clay, molds and stamps for working with clay, and molded and stamped clay pieces

Basic Supplies

Polymer clay

Acrylic roller or a pasta machine used exclusively for polymer clay

Plastic molding sticks

Polymer clay knife

Decorative molds for use with polymer clay

Ceramic tile (working surface)

TIPS FOR WORKING WITH POLYMER CLAY

- Always condition the clay before trying to mold it. Work it until it warms up and becomes more pliable.

- A pasta machine makes conditioning and rolling out clay easier and faster. It is a wise investment if you enjoy creating with this medium. CAUTION: Once you use a pasta machine for polymer clay, it **cannot** be used for food preparation.

- A light dusting of cornstarch in decorative molds prevents the clay from sticking.

- To be sure polymer clay pieces adhere to the slick surface of a jar, brush a thin coat of white glue on the back of the clay piece before placing on the jar.

Jar Embellishments

Embellishments make your jars look professional and finished. These are some of my favorites.

Labels

You'll find a wide variety of pre-printed, self-adhesive labels at crafts, department, and office supply stores for decorating jars, lids, and gift tags. Before applying, make sure your jar surface is clean and grease-free. Some labels need to wrap around the jar and stick to themselves to prevent the label from pulling away from the jar.

You can design your own labels with photographs and printed motifs on double-sided adhesive paper or with a laminating machine. (The machine is especially handy if you're making and decorating lots of jars for gifts or to sell.)

Wire & Beads

You'll find a large assortment of beautiful glass, plastic, ceramic, and bone beads and colored wire to decorate your jars. Choose 20 gauge or 22 gauge wire – both sizes are easy to work with and hold shapes well. Use 18-gauge wire for creating handles on jars.

Beads also can be added to cords (elastic or not), ribbons, or tassels. Beautiful and inexpensive beaded trims are easy to find and offer great embellishment possibilities.

Ribbons & Trims

Ribbons and trims like braid, fringe, cord, string, raffia, and twill tape are easy to work with. A huge variety of widths, colors and textures awaits your creative touch.

Charms & Buttons

Charms are available in a range of metallic finishes and painted motifs. Use silicone-based glue designed for metal to adhere charms to the jars and lids.

Plastic and metal buttons of all types can be used to decorate jars. Use wire cutters to remove the metal shanks before gluing the buttons with silicon-based glue.

Tassels

Fabric stores, home decor outlets, and craft stores stock lots of sizes and colors of tassels. You can make plain tassels more elaborate by adding fused pearls, ribbon roses, or charms.

For a custom look, make your own tassels from cord and lampshade fringe. (You can also use beads, ribbon pieces, or yarn.) Here's how to make two tassels:

1. Cut a 20" piece cord and two pieces, each 4" long, of 3-1/2" lampshade fringe.
2. Loop and knot each end of the cord. Place a line of glue along the top edges of the fringe pieces.
3. Tightly wrap the fringe around the cord ends, leaving a 1" loop. Let dry. Trim the cord to the length of the fringe.
4. Embellish the tassels with fused pearl trim and a gold ribbon rose.

Decorated Jar Projects

Whether you want to make a jar to give as a gift or to use for storage or as a room accent, you'll find a wealth of ideas and inspirations on the pages that follow.

Starting from the top, you'll find information about decorating tops and making labels and tags. You'll see a variety of painted jar projects that are both useful and decorative. You'll find decoupage projects, including altered art collage jars and ones with lace and fabric trims. There are jars decorated with polymer clay, jars topped with critter faces that are sure to bring a smile, memory jars, and decorative arrangements.

As no jar collection would be complete without ideas for food gifts, you'll find those as well, with ingredient lists for filling and recipes for giving.

Enjoy them all!

JAR TOPPERS

A beautifully adorned lid can be part of a jar's decorating theme or the jar's single decorative element. Lids can be decorated with a variety of materials – paper, fabric, lace, three-dimensional arrangements, beads, and silk flowers are just a few. The lid can extend or create a mood (glitzy, dramatic, romantic) or embody a decorating style (Victorian, country, beach). The following pages show an array of inspirational examples.

Paper-Topped Lids

Paper is an easy way to cover a lid. For a coordinated presentation, look for decorative papers with matching border stickers and accent stickers at craft stores. You can also use up small bits and pieces left over from scrapbooking on lids. Decorative paper circles are a great way to top recycled jar lids and cover printing.

Basic Supplies for Paper-Topped Lids
• Papers – Decorative papers, card papers
• Trims & embellishments – Border stickers, strips of matching paper, accent stickers, rub-on motifs, novelty buttons
• Circle template and shape cutter
• Paper trimmer
• Glue gun with clear glue sticks

Basic Instructions for Paper-Topped Lids
For a flat lid and screw-on band
1. Use the circle template and shape cutter to cut out a circle from decorative or card paper. With the glue gun, stick the paper circle to the top of the flat lid.
2. Cut a 1/2" strip from a piece of decorative paper with the paper trimmer. Glue around the rim of the band. *Option:* Use border stickers.
3. Accent further with stickers or rub-on motifs. ❏

Pictured clockwise from top left:
• Lace doily attached to top with ribbon woven through doily;
• paper top with coordinating label;
• fabric top with ribbon-covered band, charms have been glued on top;
• padded fabric top with jute trim;
• birdhouse and nest three-dimensional arrangement glued on top of lid, the ring is decorated with a raffia tie;
• padded fabric top with lace trim glued around ring.

CHICKEN NOODLE SOUP

- 1 jar **Chicken Noodle Soup Mix**
- 8 cups water
- 2 carrots, diced
- 2 stalks celery, diced
- ¼ cup minced onion
- 3 cup cooked chicken

Simmer all ingredients except the meat for about 15 minutes. Add the meat in last 5 minutes of cooking.

Love Mom

Love the Brownings

Fabric-Topped Lids

Fabric-topped lids are easy, traditional toppers for food gifts. With the simple trims and embellishments, your jars go from ordinary to extraordinary. Use cotton fabrics or cotton-polyester blends for best results.

Basic Supplies for Fabric-Topped Lids
• Fabric – squares or circle shapes, 5" for standard jars, 6" for wide-mouth jars
• Trims & embellishments – Ribbon, lace, jute or raffia; charms, flat buttons, or novelty buttons with shanks removed
• Polyester batting, *optional* – for a puffy lid

• Glue gun with clear glue sticks
• Scissors

Basic Instructions for Fabric-Topped Lids
1. *Option:* Use the flat lid as a template to cut a piece of batting. Glue to the top of the lid with a glue gun.
2. Place the flat lid on the jar. Place the square or circle of fabric, centered on top.
3. Twist on the metal band to hold everything in place.
4. With the glue gun, add the matching trim and embellishments

Puffy fabric-topped lids.

Flat fabric-topped lid.

Lace-Topped Lids

Crocheted and lace-edged doilies lend a romantic touch to jar lids. You can buy new doilies or look for antique ones at thrift shops and tag sales. (I find them regularly for less than a dollar.) I especially like doilies with linen centers and am always on the lookout for clean ones in good condition. You can also cut up stained or damaged doilies and use the pieces to cover a flat lid. The screw-on band hides the cut edges.

Basic Supplies for Lace-Topped Lids
• Doilies, old or new, 6" to 7" diameter
• Trims & embellishments – Ribbons, lace, crocheted flowers, silk flowers, buttons, jewels, charms
• Polyester batting, *optional* – for a puffy lid
• Glue gun with clear glue sticks

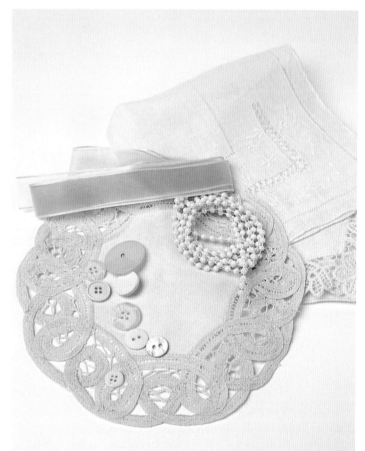

Supplies for Lace-Topped Lids

Pictured at left: A lace-trimmed doily embellished with a crocheted flower and embroidered leaf makes a feminine topper for a jar of bath salts. A piece of white fabric is glued to the metal jar lid. The greeting on the pink-bordered label was written with a pink gel pen.

The wire mesh top, *right,* is the ideal lid for a jar filled with potpourri or a decorated jar to be used as a vase. (The wire mesh holds the flower stems in place for a perfect arrangement.) Using the flat lid as a template, cut out a circle of metal mesh with wire shears. Place the mesh circle inside the screw-on band and form a dome with your hands. Screw the band on the jar to hold the wire mesh in place. Tie ribbons around the band for color.

Basic Instructions for Lace-Topped Lids

Using a doily with a flat lid and screw-on band

1. *Option:* Use the flat lid as a template to cut a piece of the polyester batting. Glue to the top of the lid with the glue gun.
2. Place the flat lid on the jar. Place the doily, centering it over the lid.
3. Twist the metal band on the jar to hold everything in place.

4. With the glue gun, add trim and embellishments.

Using a doily as a lid

This is an excellent cover for a jar filled with fragrant potpourri or gel.

1. Omit the flat lid and place a doily over the band.
2. Thread a piece of ribbon through the lacy doily and tie it snugly around the band.
3. Trim with a silk rose.

Three-Dimensional Arrangements on Lids

All kinds of miniature items can be used to compose three-dimensional arrangements on jar lids that will turn a simple jar into a special hostess gift. Use the arrangements to extend a theme, like the shells, netting, and rope on the Beach Cottage Jar, or as a tabletop embellishment for a jar of jam or honey. Use a mini garland to evoke a holiday mood.

On the Beach Cottage Jar, a blue-edged label is decorated with a single tiny shell.

Bird's Nest Honey Jar, Berries & Ladybug Jam Jar

Basic Supplies for Three-Dimensional Arrangements
- Base – Felt, fabric, or paper circles to cover flat lids
- Arrangement elements – Shells, miniature novelty pieces, beads, silk and artificial flowers and fruits, miniature garlands
- Trims & embellishments – Charms, ribbon, raffia, cord
- Glue gun with clear glue sticks
- White craft glue

Fancy Tops for Jars of Sweet Treats

For the Daisies Galore Jar, *left,* the flat lid was first glued inside the screw-on band, then covered with silk daisies. Ribbon and pearls circle the band. For the matching tag, a tag template and shape cutter were used to cut a tag from card paper. A silk daisy was glued to the tag and 12" of gold elastic cord was threaded through a punched reinforced with a paper circle.

On the Holiday Garland Jar, *below left,* the flat lid is covered with a circle of green felt and a mini garland is glued around the rim. To make the Beaded Top Jar, *below right,* glue the flat lid into the band with silicone-based glue and let dry. Spread white craft glue over the entire top and sides of the lid and sprinkle beads on the wet glue. When dry, add an acrylic gem to the lid center.

Basic Instructions

1. Cover the flat lid with a piece of felt, paper, or fabric.

2. Glue the lid inside the screw-on band.

3. Arrange the pieces and glue in place.

4. Add trim and embellishments. ❏

MAKING LABELS & TAGS

Use labels and tags to identify the recipient or contents of a jar, provide instructions, and add a greeting. You can make labels and tags from just about any kind of paper (a great way of using left over bits and pieces!) or choose from the huge array of beautiful blank and decorative self-adhesive labels available at crafts, stationery, and art supply stores.

When designing your tags and labels, keep the theme of the jar design by using the same materials that you used to decorate the lid or jar. Accent labels and tags with decorative stickers or lettering and attach them to the jar itself or use ribbon, cord, or raffia tied around the neck of the jar. For an extra decorative touch, use thin elastic cord that has been strung with beads.

Basic Supplies for Tags & Labels

- Papers – Card paper, decorative paper
- Trims & embellishments – Stickers, self-adhesive labels, ribbon, elastic cord, raffia, beads
- Decorative-edge scissors
- Tag template and shape cutter
- Hole punches
- Felt markers or gel pens
- Glue stick
- Glue gun and clear glue sticks

TAG TIPS

- A tag template with a shape cutter is great for cutting out tags from decorative paper – you can make lots of tags easily.

- When using lightweight decorative paper for a tag, glue it to a piece of heavier card paper and trim with decorative scissors.

- Use decorative-edge scissors to cut interesting edges on layered paper panels.

- Write greetings and lettering with gel pens or felt pens.

- Use a variety of hole punch shapes and eyelets for attaching the tags to jars with elastic cord or ribbon.

Fruit Gift Tags

Fruit stickers were used to embellish these metal-rimmed vellum tags. A 2" x 4" piece of cream card paper was folded in half and attached to the back. Sheer ribbon was threaded through the punched holes to tie the tags to the jars.

Watermelon Label & Lid

Reproductions of an antique fruit crate labels are easy finishing touches for a jar of homemade jam. A purchased tag was decorated with stickers, and 15" of green jute cord was threaded through the hole to tie the tag to the jar. A watermelon slice novelty button, with the shank removed, is glued on the lid as a three-dimensional accent.

Patterns
(actual size)

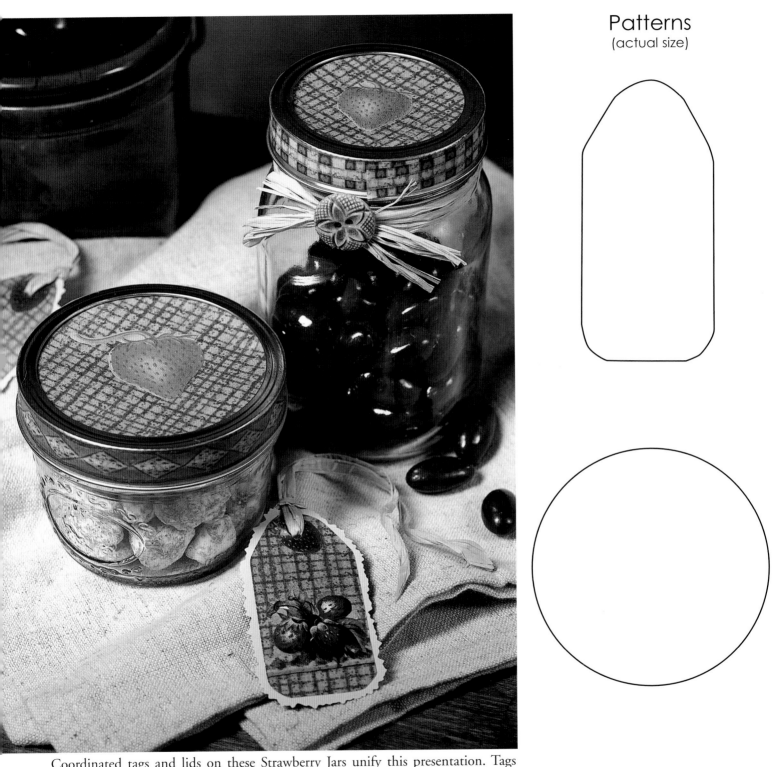

Coordinated tags and lids on these Strawberry Jars unify this presentation. Tags were cut from decorative paper, glued to tan card paper, and trimmed with deckle edge scissors. Strawberry and border stickers decorate the tags, which are attached with lengths of natural raffia. The flat lids have matching paper covers and strawberry stickers; different border stickers cover the screw-on bands.

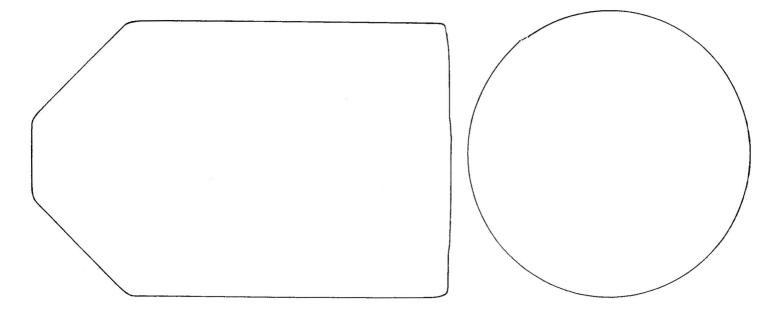

In the Dragonfly Jar, *left,* the sticker-decorated jar holds a tissue-wrapped gift. For the Butterfly Jar, *right,* a tag was cut from card paper, decorated with stickers, and attached with 10" of gold elastic cord strung with a dozen glass beads.

CITRUS TRIO
painted jars

These lemon, lime, and orange jars are painted in a quick, whimsical style with bright, cheerful colors. The black-and-white ribbon trim complements the black outlines, lettering, and details, which are added with a paint pen. Fun lids with miniature fruits top off the retro-look storage jars.

JAR TYPE

Three quart-size canning jars with screw-on bands and flat metal seals

SUPPLIES FOR PAINTING

Acrylic enamel paints for glass – White, orange, lime green, yellow, medium green

Acrylic paints for metal – Orange, lime green, yellow

Fine point paint pen – Black

Tracing paper and pencil

Transfer paper and stylus

Artist's paint brushes – 1" flat, #4 flat, #3 round, 1/2" flat

plus Basic painting supplies

EMBELLISHMENTS

Mini artificial fruits – Lemon, lime, orange

3 yds. black and white checked ribbon

3 black buttons

Needle and black thread

OTHER SUPPLIES

Rubber band

Silicone glue

Glue gun and clear glue stick

Two-part resin coating and basic supplies for coating

JAR DECORATION

Turn the page to see the Lemon Painting Guide.

1. Basecoat the outsides of the jars with white acrylic enamel, using a 1" brush. Let dry completely.
2. Trace the patterns on tracing paper.
3. Transfer the motifs to the jars with transfer paper.
4. Paint the fruits and leaves with acrylic enamels, using a #4 flat brush. (Worksheet, Fig. 1) TIP: Don't worry about blending the colors or softening your brush strokes – you want a whimsical look. Let dry completely.
5. Create a fun upper border by writing the name of the fruit around the top of the jar, using a black paint pen. TIP: Keep the border straight by placing a rubber band around the jar where you want the border to be. Use the rubber band as a painting guide. When completely dry, remove the rubber band to reveal a perfectly straight border.
6. Lightly pencil a wavy line around the bottom of each jar to mark the placement of the bottom border.
7. Paint green leaves on the border, using a #3 round brush. (Worksheet, Fig. 2) Let dry.
8. Outline the leaves the black paint pen.
9. Add details and outlines to the fruits with the black paint pen. (Worksheet, Fig. 2)
10. Follow manufacturer's instructions for curing and care.

Continued on page 40

continued from page 40

LID DECORATION

1. Glue the flat lids in the screw bands using a silicone-based glue for metal. Let the glue dry and cure completely.
2. Paint the entire lid surface with acrylic metal paints, using a different color for each lid and a 1/2" flat brush.
3. Using silicone-based glue, adhere the miniature fruits in the center of each lid.
4. Coat the top of the lid with a two-part resin, following the instructions in the Supplies & Techniques section. Pour the resin carefully into the well at the top of the lid, over the fruit, and use a disposable brush to make sure the fruits are completely covered. Let the lids cure 24 hours before placing on the painted jars.

EMBELLISHMENTS

1. Cut three 20" pieces of ribbon. Tie one piece around the neck of each jar, leaving two tails. Trim the ends of the tails in V-shapes.
2. With the remaining ribbon, make three two-loop tailored bows. Secure with a black button at the center of each, using a needle and thread.
3. Using a glue gun, glue the bows to the ribbons on the jars. ❏

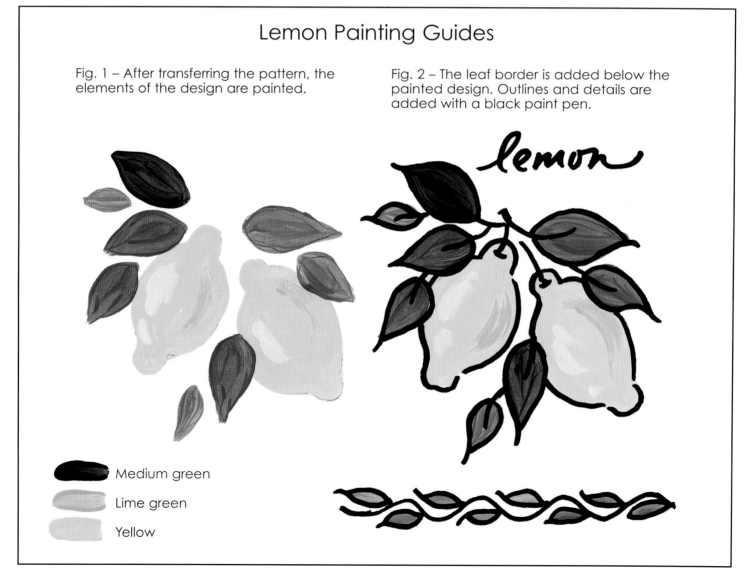

Lemon Painting Guides

Fig. 1 – After transferring the pattern, the elements of the design are painted.

Fig. 2 – The leaf border is added below the painted design. Outlines and details are added with a black paint pen.

Medium green

Lime green

Yellow

Lemon

Patterns
(actual size)

Lime

Orange

FIELDS OF LAVENDER
painted jar

This painted jar was designed to hold a bouquet of silk flowers as an everlasting arrangement to accent French country decor. CAUTION: The inside of this jar is painted – **DO NOT** use with food. If you wish to use the jar with food, do not paint the inside. If you wish the jar to hold food or freshly cut flowers, spray the basecoat on the **outside** of the jar before painting the design.

JAR TYPE

Recycled mayonnaise jar with wide metal screw band

PAINTING SUPPLIES

Spray paint – Light blue

Acrylic enamel paint for glass – Lilac, light blue, pale green, sage green, medium green

Acrylic paints for metal – Sage green (to paint lid)

Fine sea sponge

Artist's paint brushes -#1 round, #4 round, #1 liner, 1/2" flat

plus Basic painting supplies

OTHER SUPPLIES

Fine sandpaper

Natural raffia

JAR DECORATION

See the Lavender Painting Guide on page 45.

1. Basecoat the inside of the jar with two coats of spray paint. Let dry.

2. Using a fine sponge with sage green paint, sponge the background foliage around the bottom of the jar.

3. Using the fine sponge with light green paint, sponge over the first layer for contrast.

4. Holding the jar upside down, use a # 1 round paintbrush to paint the lavender stalks. Space them 1/2" to 1" apart and make them a variety of lengths.

5. Using a #4 round brush with lilac paint, add blossoms to the top of each stalk.

6. Add blue accents to the blossoms.

7. Holding the jar upside down and stroking toward you, add the green leaves.

8. Follow the manufacturer's instructions for curing and care.

LID DECORATION

Paint the metal ring with the sage green paint for metal, using a 1/2" flat brush. Let dry.

EMBELLISHMENTS

1. Place the screw band on the jar.

2. Tie natural raffia below the band. ❏

FIELDS OF WHEAT
painted jar

This painted jar is designed to hold a candle or a bouquet of silk flowers for an everlasting arrangement to accent a room with farm country decor. CAUTION: The inside of this jar is painted – **DO NOT** use with food. If you wish to use the jar with food, do not paint the inside. If you wish the jar to hold food or freshly cut flowers, spray the basecoat on the **outside** of the jar before painting the design.

Pictured on page 43

Pictured on page 43

JAR TYPE

Recycled mayonnaise jar with wide metal screw band

Option: Clear glass "flower pot" votive with candle

PAINTING SUPPLIES

Spray paint – Light blue

Acrylic enamel paint for glass – Yellow, burnt orange

Acrylic paints for metal – Cream

Fine sea sponge

Artist's paint brushes -#1 round, #4 round, #1 liner, 1/2" flat

plus Basic painting supplies

OTHER SUPPLIES

Fine sandpaper

Natural raffia

JAR DECORATION

See the Wheat Painting Worksheet.

1. Basecoat the inside of the jar with two coats of spray paint. Let dry.

2. Using a 1" flat brush with yellow paint, add quick brush strokes along the bottom of the jar to create the background. TIP: Hold the jar upside down and bring the strokes towards you.

3. Mix yellow and burnt orange to create a medium hue. Using a #1 round paintbrush and holding the jar upside down, paint the wheat stalks, spacing them about 1/2" apart in a variety of lengths.

4. With a #4 round brush and the medium hue mix, paint wheat berries at the top of each stalk.

5. Holding the jar upside down and pulling the paint strokes towards you, add burnt orange leaves.

6. Add small, thin accent strokes to each wheat berry, using a #1 liner brush.

7. Follow the manufacturer's instructions for curing and care.

LID DECORATION

1. Paint the metal band with the acrylic metal paint, using a 1/2" flat brush. Let dry.

2. Rub the band with fine sandpaper to give a distressed, antique character.

EMBELLISHMENTS

1. Place the screw band on the jar.

2. Tie natural raffia below the band. ❏

Yellow

Medium hue
(yellow + burnt
orange)

Burnt orange

Wheat Painting Guides

Light blue

Lilac

Sage green

Pale green

Medium green

Lavender Painting Guides

WILD SPOTS & STRIPES
painted jars

These jars are painted with stripes or spots that mimic animal prints.
They are easy to paint and perfect to use as vases or for storage.
Using acrylic enamels allows you to wash the jars.

JAR TYPE

4 quart-size canning jars with wide or standard openings

PAINTING SUPPLIES

Acrylic enamel paints for glass – Cream, tan, orange, black

Artist's paint brushes – 1" basecoating, #4 round, 1/4" deerfoot, 3/8" deerfoot

Flat sponge

plus Basic painting supplies

OTHER SUPPLIES

Natural raffia

Novelty buttons (African mask or animal motifs), shanks removed

Glue gun and clear glue sticks

JAR DECORATION

Tiger Jar:
1. Basecoat the outside of the jar with orange, using a 1" brush.
2. While still wet, use a flat sponge to add a light horizontal shading to the top and bottom of the jar with brown.
3. Add thick and thin stripes with black paint.
4. Follow the manufacturer's instructions for curing and care.

Zebra Jar:
See the zebra painting guide on page 48.
1. Basecoat the outside of the jar with cream, using a 1" brush.
2. While still wet, use a flat sponge to add a light horizontal shading to the top and bottom of the jar with brown.
3. Add thick and thin stripes with black paint, using a #4 round brush.
4. Follow the manufacturer's instructions for curing and care.

Leopard Jar:
See the leopard painting guide on page 48.
1. Basecoat the outside of the jar with cream.
2. While still wet, use a flat sponge to add vertical bands of light shading 2" apart around the jar with brown.
3. Use the large and small deerfoot brushes to add irregular spots with orange.
4. Outline the spots with black.
5. Follow the manufacturer's instructions for curing and care.

Jaguar Jar:
1. Basecoat the outside of the jar with tan.
2. While still wet, use a flat sponge to add vertical bands of light shading 2" apart around the jar with brown.
3. Use the large and small deerfoot brushes to add irregular spots with black.
4. Follow the manufacturer's instructions for curing and care.

EMBELLISHMENTS

1. Cut a 24" piece of natural raffia. Wrap around the neck of the jar and knot in the front.
2. Glue a novelty button in the middle of the knot. ❏

Pictured left to right, opposite: Leopard Jar, Tiger Jar, Jaguar Jar, Zebra Jar

Leopard Painting Guide

Zebra Painting Guide

COFFEE TIME
painted jar with resin-coated lid

This jar is the perfect vessel to hold coffee in the break room or to fill with beans as part of a coffee lover's gift basket. Paint pens were used to embellish a coffee-colored painted band. The top is decorated with real coffee beans and coated with resin.

JAR TYPE
Wire, bail acrylic storage jar

PAINTING SUPPLIES
Acrylic enamel paints for glass – Brown

Paint pens – Gold, silver

Artist's paint brushes – #10 flat, #3 round

plus Basic painting supplies

OTHER SUPPLIES
White glue

Two-part resin coating and general coating supplies

Jute garden cord

Glue gun and clear glue stick

JAR DECORATION
1. Using the #10 flat brush with brown acrylic enamel, paint a wavy band around the middle of the jar.
2. Paint small ovals, which will become the coffee beans, over and under the band with a #3 round brush. Let dry completely.
3. With the gold and silver paint pens, add swirls and dots. Use the gold pen to write "Coffee Time" on the band, to outline the band, and to add details to the painted coffee beans. TIP: A piece of dark colored paper inside the jar will help you see what the design will look like when filled with dark coffee beans.

LID DECORATION
1. Glue the coffee beans in a spiral to the top of the lid, using white craft glue. Let dry completely.
2. Cover the indented area of the lid with a two-part resin coating. See "Coating Jars & Lids with Resin" in the Supplies & Techniques section. TIP: Applying resin only to the center of the lid will keep the resin from flowing over the sides.

EMBELLISHMENTS
Glue jute garden string around the top of the jar using a glue gun and clear glue sticks. ❑

SIMPLE ROSES
painted jars

You don't need a pattern to paint these super-simple rose designs that adorn the painted stripes and oval "label." Use the jars to hold a bouquet of flowers or for storage. Using acrylic enamels allows you to wash the jars.

JAR TYPE

3 quart-size canning jars

PAINTING SUPPLIES

Acrylic enamel paints for glass – cream, light green, light rose, burgundy, dark green

Artist's paint brushes – 1" flat, #6 round, #3 round

plus Basic painting supplies

OTHER SUPPLIES

Rubber band

Lace trim

Small ribbon bows or ribbon flowers

Glue gun and glue sticks

JAR DECORATION

1. Basecoat the outsides of the jars with cream acrylic enamel, using a 1" brush. Let dry completely.

2. Using the photo as a guide, paint vertical or horizontal stripes or a "label" frame with light green.

3. Paint light rose flower shapes about 1/2" in diameter and 1" apart along the green stripes or around the label band.

4. Using the #3 round brush, add a few burgundy strokes to one side of each rose. Add a dot in the center.

5. Add strokes with cream to the other side of each rose.

6. Using the #6 round brush, add 4 or 5 leaves to the sides of the roses.

7. Highlight the leaves with touches of light green.

8. To create the decorative border, use the handle end of your paint brush to add cream dots along the edges of the stripes or the inside edge of the label band.

9. Add light green dots between the cream dots.

10. Follow the manufacturer's instructions for curing and care.

EMBELLISHMENTS

1. Glue cream lace trim around the top of each jar.

2. Add a ribbon bow or flower accent. ❏

Rose Paiting Guide

BLUEBERRIES
painted jar

This jar and the two that follow are perfect projects for a group or for beginning painters – you use your fingers and simple sponge shapes. TIP: Pop-up sponges are easy to cut into shapes while they are flat. Place them in water to make the shape pop up, and they're ready to use. A liner brush is used to paint the stems and branches. Using acrylic enamels for painting the jars allows the jars to be washed.

Pattern on page 55

JAR TYPE

Quart-size canning jar

PAINTING SUPPLIES

Acrylic enamel paints for glass – White, light muted blue, brown, purple, dark blue, light green, dark green

Artist's paint brushes – #1 liner, 1" flat

Compressed pop-up sponge (for leaves)

plus Basic painting supplies

OTHER SUPPLIES

Scissors

Twisted paper ribbon – Dark brown

Glue gun and clear glue sticks

JAR DECORATION

See the Blueberries Painting Guide on page 54.

1. Basecoat the outside of the jar with white acrylic enamel, using a 1" brush. Let dry completely.

2. Trace the leaf shape and transfer to the compressed pop-up sponge. Cut out the leaf shape, using scissors.

3. Paint the jar with light muted blue. Let dry.

4. Using the liner brush with brown paint, paint three to four wavy lines around the jar 2" from the top for the branches.

5. Dip your finger in dark blue, purple, or light green paints and touch on the jar to create different sizes of berries clustered around the branches. Use darker blue or purple for the larger, riper berries; smaller berries are still a bit green.

6. Wet the compressed sponge shape to expand. Squeeze out excess water. Dip in light green and dark green paints, pounce to blend, and stamp the leaves, using the photo as a guide.

7. Using a liner brush, paint brown stems to join the leaves and the berries to the branches.

8. Using a liner brush with the berry colors, paint blossoms on the ends of the berries opposite the stems.

9. Use the handle end of the brush to add a small white highlight dot to each berry. Let dry completely.

10. Follow the manufacturer's instructions for curing and care.

EMBELLISHMENTS

Cut a length of twisted paper ribbon. Wrap around the neck of the jar four or five times. Secure with glue. ❏

Blueberries Painting Guide

Grapes Painting Guide

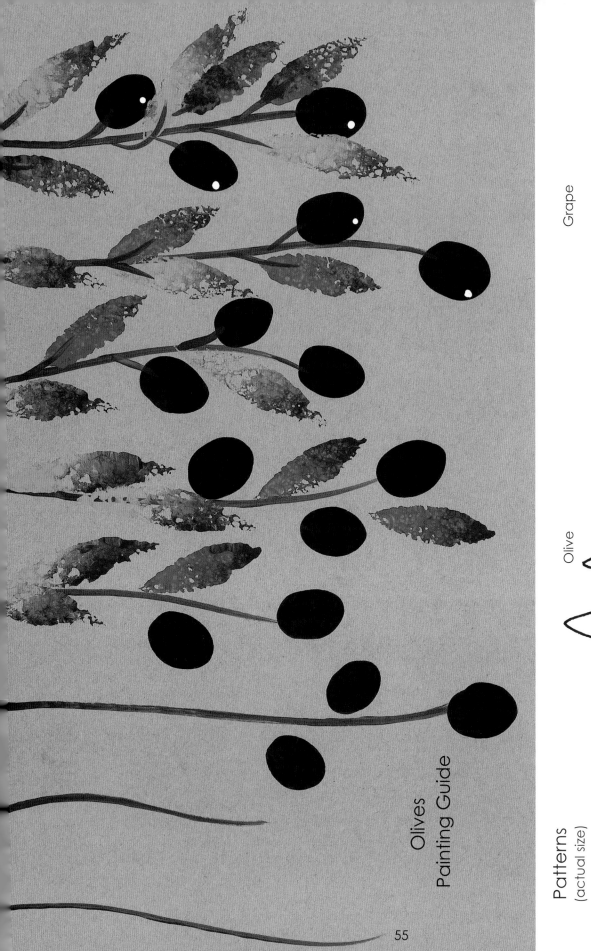

Olives
Painting Guide

Grape

Olive

Blueberry

Patterns
(actual size)

GRAPES
painted jar

JAR TYPE
Quart-size canning jar

PAINTING SUPPLIES
Acrylic enamel paints for glass – White, tan, brown, purple, light green, dark green

Artist's paint brushes – 1" flat, #1 liner

Compressed pop-up sponge (for leaves)

plus Basic painting supplies

OTHER SUPPLIES
Twisted paper – Dark brown

Glue gun and clear glue sticks

JAR DECORATION
1. Basecoat the outside of the jar with white acrylic enamel, using a 1" brush. Let dry completely.
2. Trace the leaf shape and transfer to the compressed pop-up sponge. Cut out the leaf shape.
3. Paint the jar with tan. Let dry.
4. Using the liner brush with brown paint, paint three or four wavy lines (for vines) around the top of the jar.
5. Squeeze puddles of purple and green paints on a disposable palette. Dip your finger in the paints and touch on the jar to create the clusters of grapes. Place the larger, riper grapes at the top of the cluster and the smaller ones (still be a bit green) at the bottom.
6. Wet the compressed sponge shape to expand. Squeeze out excess water. Dip in light green and dark green paints, pounce to blend, and stamp the leaves, using the photo as a guide.
7. Use the liner brush with brown paint to add stems to join the leaves and grapes to the vines. Add a few tendrils.
8. Highlight the grapes with small white dots, using the handle end of the liner brush. Let dry completely.
9. Follow the manufacturer's instructions for curing and care.

EMBELLISHMENTS
Cut a length of twisted paper ribbon. Wrap around the neck of the jar four or five times. Secure with glue. ❏

OLIVES
Painted Jar

JAR TYPE
Quart-size canning jar

PAINTING SUPPLIES
Acrylic enamel paints for glass – White, khaki green, brown, purple, black, light green, medium green

Artist's paint brushes, 1" flat, #1 liner

Compressed pop-up sponge (for leaves)

plus Basic painting supplies

OTHER SUPPLIES
Twisted paper ribbon – Dark brown

Glue gun and clear glue sticks

JAR DECORATION
1. Basecoat the outside of the jar with white acrylic enamel, using a 1" brush. Let dry completely.
2. Trace the leaf shape and transfer to the compressed pop-up sponge. Cut out the leaf shape.
3. Paint the jar with khaki green. Let dry.
4. Using the liner brush with brown paint, paint vertical, slightly wavy branches of different lengths around the jar. Space the lines about 1" apart.
5. Squeeze puddles of purple and black paints on a disposable palette. Dip your finger in the paints and touch on the jar to create the oval olives around the stems. Create the oval shape by moving your finger up and down slightly.
6. Wet the compressed sponge shape to expand. Dip in light green and medium green paints, pounce to blend, and stamp the leaves, using the photo as a guide.
7. Use a liner brush to add brown stems to join the leaves and olives to the branches.
8. Highlight the olives with small white dots, using the handle end of the liner brush. Let dry completely.
9. Follow manufacturer's instructions for curing and care.

EMBELLISHMENTS
Cut a length of twisted paper ribbon. Wrap around the neck of the jar four or five times. Secure with glue. ❏

PLAID HAPPY
painted jars

These bright painted jars hold a glass candle holder and votive candles. No patterns are needed – the handpainted, slightly askew lines add to the whimsical effect, so don't worry if your lines are not perfect! Use for decoration only if using dimensional paint. If you wish the paint to be permanent and able to be washed, use only acrylic enamels.

JAR TYPE

2 quart-size canning jars

2 clear glass votive candle holders

PAINTING SUPPLIES

For the Green & Blue Jar

Acrylic enamel paints for glass – Turquoise, lime green, bright yellow

Dimensional paints: Turquoise, metallic green

For the Purple & Pink Jar

Acrylic enamel paints for glass – lilac, jade green, dark purple

Dimensional paints – Purple, dark pink

Artist's paint brushes – 1" flat, 1/2" flat, #4 flat

plus Basic painting supplies

Other Supplies:

Rick-rack trim, wide and narrow (in colors to match paint colors)

Glue gun and clear glue sticks

White votive candles

JAR DECORATION

See the Plaid Painting Guide on page 60.

1. Using a 1" flat brush, paint wide vertical stripes around the jar, 1" apart. Let dry.

2. Using the 1/2" flat brush, add horizontal around the jar, 1" apart. Let dry.

3. Using the #4 flat brush, add thin vertical lines between the wide vertical stripes. Let dry.

4. With dimensional paint, add a wavy line to the smaller vertical stripe, outline the wide vertical stripe, and add a straight line at the middle of the wide vertical stripe.

EMBELLISHMENTS

1. Glue wide rick-rack trim around the top of the jar.

2. Glue narrow rick-rack at the center of the wide rick-rack.

3. Place candle holder in jar. Place candle in holder. ❑

Plaid Happy Painting Guide

Instructions on page 58

Tapestry Lamps Painting Guide

Instructions on page 62

TAPESTRY LAMPS
painted jars

Here's another simple painting technique that yields sophisticated results.
Rich colors and gold accents create an opulent look.

JAR TYPE

2 quart-size canning jars with standard openings

PAINTING SUPPLIES

Acrylic enamel paints for glass – Yellow, orange, purple, dark blue, burgundy, dark green

Paint pen – Fine point gold

Spray paint – gold

Artist's paint brushes – 1/2" flat, #4 round

plus Basic painting supplies

OTHER SUPPLIES

2 lamp lid kits

Metallic gold trim, 10" per jar

Beaded trim, 10" per jar

Glue gun and clear glue sticks

JAR DECORATION

1. Using the 1/2" flat brush, paint vertical stripes around the jars 1/4" apart. TIP: Have a container of water and an old towel handy to clean the brush between each color. Squeeze out all excess water from the brush before each use.

2. While the painted stripes are still wet, add more stripes between them, letting the paint colors blend and mix together. Make all brush strokes vertical ones. Let dry.

3. Use the #4 round brush to add thin stripes of various colors around the jars, using the photo as a guide. Let dry completely.

4. With the gold paint pen, add curlicues, lines, stripes, and diamonds to the jars.

5. Follow manufacturer's instructions for curing and care.

LID DECORATION

Spray the lamp kit lids with gold paint. Let dry. Place on the jars.

EMBELLISHMENTS

Glue the beaded trim and the gold trim around the necks of the jars. ❏

DRAGONFLY LIGHTS
painted jars

These candle holder jars are basecoated on the inside with spray paint and stenciled on the outside with acrylic enamels. Silver dragonflies are painted with metallic acrylic enamel paints. Two lids are glued together and sprayed silver to form holders for pillar candles. TIP: Fill the jars with sand for additional stability.

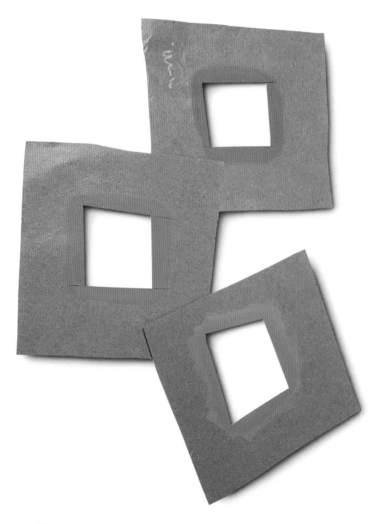

The stencils

JAR TYPE

Tall, narrow canning jars with straight sides, various heights

3 flat lids

6 lid bands

PAINTING SUPPLIES

Spray paints – Silver, jade green, light blue, sage green

Acrylic enamel paints for glass – Light blue, jade green, turquoise, metallic silver

Artist's paint brushes – #4 round, #1 liner

OTHER SUPPLIES

Freezer paper

Cutting mat and craft knife

Dense foam sponge

Silicone-based glue for metal

22 gauge green wire – 30" per jar

Blue and green glass beads – 50 per jar

Pillar candles

JAR DECORATION

1. Spray the insides of the jars with the blue and green spray paints. You may need to apply two coats for complete coverage. Let dry.
2. Using the patterns provided, cut a stencil from freezer paper.

Continued on page 66

continued from page 64

3. Using a make-up sponge, stencil the lopsided squares on the sides of the jars with the blue and green acrylic enamels. Overlap some of the shapes. Let dry.

4. See the Dragonfly Painting Worksheet, below. Using a #4 round brush, paint the dragonfly bodies (Fig. 1) and wings (Fig. 2) with silver paint. Add dots for the eyes. (Fig. 3) Use the liner brush to add curly antennae. (Fig. 4) Let dry.

LID DECORATION

1. Glue a metal lid in each of three bands.
2. Glue a second ring upside down on the first ring (the one with a lid). Let the glue dry.
3. Spray the lid assemblies with silver spray paint. Let dry. Place the lids on the jars.

EMBELLISHMENTS

1. String a 30" length of 22 gauge green wire with approximately 50 blue and green beads. Curl the ends for a decorative touch and to secure the beads.
2. Wrap the beaded wire around the jar twice and twist to hold at the front of the jar.
3. Add the candles. ❏

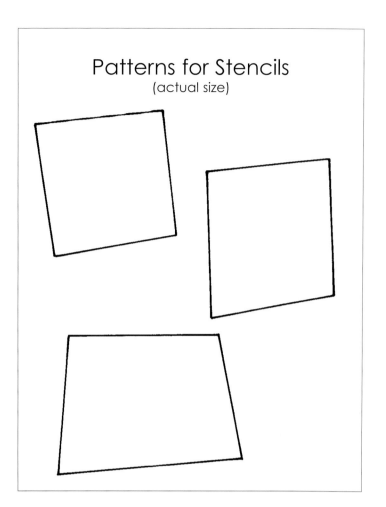

Patterns for Stencils
(actual size)

Dragonfly Painting Worksheet

Fig. 1   Fig. 2   Fig. 3   Fig. 4

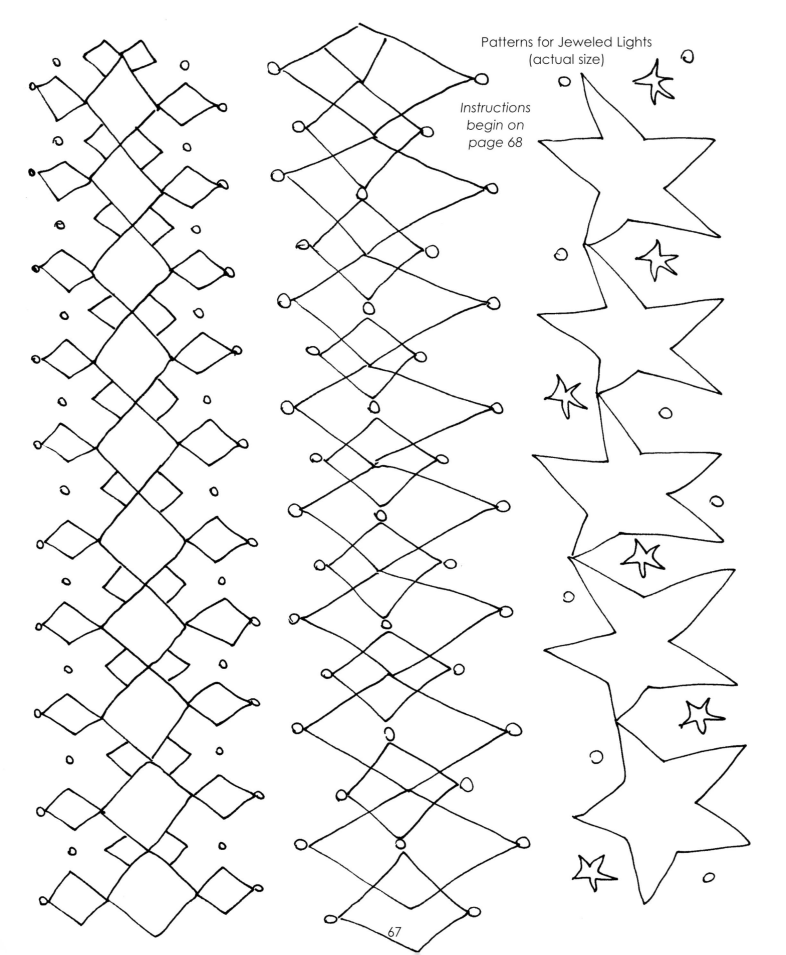

Patterns for Jeweled Lights
(actual size)

*Instructions
begin on
page 68*

JEWELED LIGHTS

painted jars

These jar lights are perfect for hanging outdoors to illuminate a summer's eve. The slightly quirky geometric shapes are simple and easy to paint. Make the wire hangers at least 8" tall to prevent the overheating from the heat of the flame.

JAR TYPE

3 pint-size canning jars

PAINTING SUPPLIES

Transparent paints for glass – Lime green, blue, emerald green, dark green

Dimensional paint *or* faux leading paint for glass – Gold

Tracing paper

Transfer paper

plus Basic painting supplies

OTHER SUPPLIES

20 gauge aluminum sheeting – one 2" x 12" strip per jar

18 gauge aluminum armature wire – one 24" piece and one 12" piece per jar

Silver paper brads – 2 per jar

Masking tape

1/8" hole punch

Metal shears

Wooden craft stick

Protective gloves, such as leather gardening gloves

JAR DECORATION

1. Trace the pattern on tracing paper. Transfer the motif to the jar with the tracing paper pattern and transfer paper.

2. With gold dimensional paint, outline the pattern. Let dry completely.

3. With blue and green transparent paints, fill in the areas inside the dimensional gold lines. Let dry.

EMBELLISHMENTS

1. Score and fold each aluminum strip to create a strip 1" wide. Use a wooden stir stick to burnish the edges and smooth them. TIP: Wear protective gloves. The edges are sharp!

2. Wrap the band into a circle 3-1/4" in diameter, overlapping the ends. It should fit over the top of the jar with a little slack.

3. Join the ends by punching two holes through the overlapping ends. Fasten with brads. Set aside.

4. Fold the 24" wire in half. Twist the top to form the loop for hanging. Curl both ends.

5. Tape the wire hanger to the jar to hold. Wrap the 12" piece of wire around the neck of the jar to hold the hanger. Twist the ends and turn the sharp ends under. Remove the tape.

6. Slip the metal band around the wire loop. Form the band around the neck of the jar to hold the hanger firmly in place. ❑

FROSTED ROSES
painted jars

These three faux etched jars are an elegant accent for a bathroom or dressing table, keeping cotton balls, cotton swabs, and make-up sponges right at your fingertips. Tape was used to mask off the designs. Mixing the opaque paint with the trasparent medium creates the etched glass effect.

JAR TYPE

3 apothecary jars with metal lids that have round knobs, variety of sizes

PAINTING SUPPLIES

Acrylic enamel paints for glass – White plus clear medium

plus Basic painting supplies

OTHER SUPPLIES

Foam make-up sponge

Low tack masking tape, 1/4", 1"

Large silk roses – 1 per jar

Sharp scissors

Clear crystal beaded trim

Clear crystal beaded tassel

Double-sided tape

JAR DECORATION

1. Use tape to mask off the striped designs. Press the tape firmly to prevent paint from seeping underneath. TIP: Carefully plan your designs so you never tape over a painted area, even if the paint is dry to the touch. The tape will pull up the paint when it is removed.
2. Make a transparent mix by adding a few drops of white paint to a 1" puddle of clear medium. TIP: Test the mix on the bottom of the jar – you want a translucent white effect.
3. Use a dense foam make-up sponge to pounce very thin coats of the paint mix to the exposed jar surface. TIP: Don't overload the sponge. Remove the tape while the paint is fresh. Set the jar aside to dry before adding a second coat.

Small jar – Simple stripes with 1/4" tape.

Large jar – Varying stripes of light frost and heavy frost. First, strips of 1" tape are spaced 1" apart. After the first coat of paint was applied, the tape was removed and 1/4" tape was added at the middle of the clear stripes. A second coat of paint was applied and the tape was removed.

Medium jar – Simple plaid stripes of various widths and frost intensities.

LID DECORATION

1. For each lid, take apart a large silk rose by pulling off the plastic center.
2. With sharp scissors, cut a 1/4" slit in each petal layer near the center hole.
3. Starting with the largest petal layer, push each layer over the knob on the jar lid. (No glue is needed.)

EMBELLISHMENTS

Finish the tops of the jars with beaded trim or a beaded tassel. Secure with the trim with clear double-sided tape. ❏

BEADED AIR FRESHENERS
painted jars

These five sparkling beaded jars are quick and easy to create. Dimensional paint is applied using the squeeze applicator on the package and tiny clear glass marbles (hole-less beads) are sprinkled on the wet paint. An acrylic faceted jewel is glued at the center of each lid for a dazzling accent. The jars are filled with jewel-toned gel air fresheners that can be scented to match the painted flower motifs. The following pages include information about coloring and scenting gel air fresheners.

With the tracing paper pattern inside the jar, dimensional paint is applied to the design lines.

Sprinkling the beads over the wet paint.

JAR TYPE

Fragrance gel jars with perforated tops and plastic liners

SUPPLIES

Dimensional paint – variety of colors

Tracing paper

Tiny clear glass marbles (hole-less beads)

Water-based fragrance gel

Acrylic gem

Glue

Disposable bowl, shoebox lid, or tray

JAR DECORATION

1. Trace the pattern on a piece of tracing paper and place inside the jar.

2. Using the photo as a guide for color placement, apply dimensional paint. TIP: Don't apply too much paint – if you do, the weight of the tiny marbles will cause the design to sag or drip.

3. Hold the jar over a bowl, a shoebox lid, or a tray. Lightly sprinkle the tiny marbles over the wet paint. Lay and prop the jars on your work surface with the painted side up until dry.

4. Fill the jar with colored, scented gel fragrance.

LID EMBELLISHMENT

Pictured above, left to right: Red Clover Jar, Rose Jar

Glue a single color-coordinated gem to the center of the lid of each jar. ❑

Making Air Freshener Jars

I've experimented with recipes for gelled air fresheners, including ones made with gelatin. I prefer to buy a gel base – the bases I tried to make grew moldy very quickly and were always cloudy, not clear.

With gel air fragrance base, you can create your own wonderful scented clear gel air fragrance. The gel base is odorless, colorless, and completely water-soluble, so you'll need water-based colorants and water-based fragrances made especially for the gel to create a successful product. (Other fragrances, such as perfumes and essential oils, will cloud the gel permanently.)

Here's How:
Using a purchased base
1. Scoop the gel from the container. Place in a heat-resistant glass measuring cup. Microwave for 1 minute on medium-high; continue heating at 15-second intervals until the gel is completely melted.
2. Add the water-soluble color tints, one drop at a time, until the desired color is achieved.
3. Add up to 1/2 ounce of water-soluble concentrated fragrance to 8 ounces gel. Stir lightly.
4. Pour the scented, colored gel into a decorative glass jar. Allow to cool until firm.

To use: Remove the plastic liner and replace the perforated lid for a soft, sweet fragrance. The air freshener releases its fragrance as the gel evaporates, and as it does, the gel volume will reduce. To rehydrate, simply add a small amount of distilled water. ❑

Patterns
(actual size)

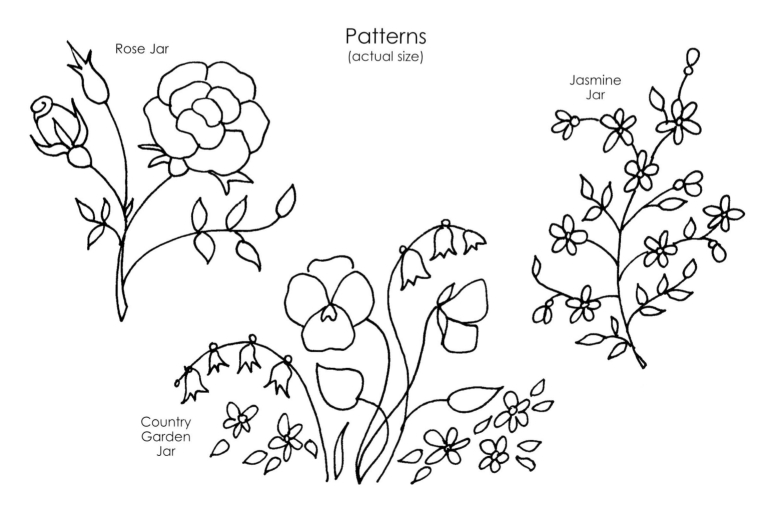

Rose Jar

Jasmine Jar

Country Garden Jar

Pictured above, clockwise from top: Jasmine Jar, Country Garden Jar, Lavender Jar

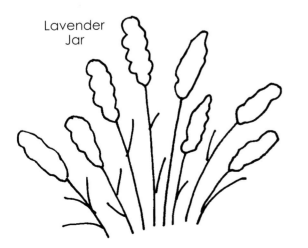

Lavender Jar

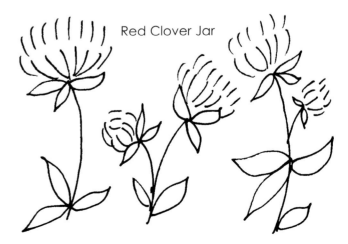

Red Clover Jar

FAUX ANTIQUE ENAMELWARE
painted jars

These jars mimic the look of vintage enamelware. Rubbing away wet paint creates the look of white enamel wearing away from black tin. The jars were designed to hold fresh flowers; add large corks to turn them into storage containers.

Patterns
(actual size)

JAR TYPE

Recycled jars with straight sides (These are salad dressing jars.)

PAINTING SUPPLIES

Dimensional paint – Black
Spray paint – White gloss

OTHER SUPPLIES

Tracing paper
Paper towels
Black and white striped ribbon – 10" per jar
Glue gun and clear glue stick

JAR DECORATION

1. Trace the patterns and place inside the jars.
2. Outline the designs with black dimensional paint. TIP: Be careful not to apply too much paint; if you do, the design could sag or drip. Lay the jars on your work surface with the painted sides up, propping them so they won't roll around, until completely dry.
3. Spray the outside of the jar with white paint. Immediately after spraying, wrap your finger in a paper towel and rub the raised design to let a small amount of the black paint show. If needed, spray again with white paint and wipe away the paint on the raised areas. TIP: Do not let the white paint dry before rubbing – spray paint is durable and hard to remove once it dries.

EMBELLISHMENTS

Cut lengths of black and white striped ribbon fit the neck of each jar. Glue in place. ❏

ALTERED ART COLLAGE
decoupaged jars

"Altered" art is another word for collage, a fine art technique where papers and found objects are glued to a surface. The jars of the next few pages are examples of collage. Use them as fancy storage on a desk, as bases to hold candles, or as wonderful gift packages. The jars were coated with a two-part resin for a professional, finished look.

I've included tips for creating altered art jars and outlined the basic steps. Above all, be creative and have fun! Don't be afraid to place items upside down, sideways, or overlapping – it's your work of art. Make it a reflection of you and your love of working with beautiful materials.

TIPS FOR CREATING ALTERED ART JARS

- Choose a theme, then work within it. A theme can be as simple as the color red, or more complicated, such as "travel to Paris." Collect images, colors, phrases, photographs, textures and ephemera that relate to your theme.

- Consider using theme collage sheets. These papers are printed with images that make interesting additions to a collage. Find them, along with many beautiful collage papers, stickers, and ephemera packages, at crafts stores or stamping and scrapbooking shops.

- The background paper should cover most of the jar. Use a thin paper, such as gift wrap, tissue, thin handmade paper, or decoupage paper, rather than heavier (card weight) paper.

- Use smaller images to create the collage. (Smaller images fit nicely on curved surfaces.)

- Paper images can be ripped, torn, or cut with a straight or decorative edge. Use a variety of edges, not all straight, not all torn.

- Think about framing paper pieces with a darker piece behind them, edging the piece with ink, or using different shapes to visually break up the composition.

- Repeating a motif, color, or accent in your composition brings everything together. Variety is good, but repeating gives rhythm to the composition.

- Use clear decoupage medium or thin bodied white glue to adhere papers to the jars.

- Accents usually are objects other than paper that bring dimension to the composition. For jars, ribbons, charms, beads, and trims can all be used. Attach them with a glue gun and clear glue sticks.

Pictured above: Retro 50s Jar.

Basic Instructions for Altered Art Jars

1. To cover a quart-size wide-mouth canning jar, cut a piece of paper 5-1/2" x 12". Cut slits with scissors, 1/2" apart, across the long top of the paper piece. **(photo 1)**

2. Apply a thin layer of decoupage medium or white glue to the entire back surface of the paper. Wrap the paper around the jar, smoothing out all the bubbles and wrinkles. The cut pieces at the top will overlap slightly over the curved shoulder of the jar, preventing large wrinkles. **(photo 2)**

3. Assemble a selection of stamped and printed images that work with your theme. Cut the decorative papers into strips or panels. Attach them to the jar with the decoupage medium. Let dry. **(photo 3)**

4. Decorate the flat lid to match the jar. **(photo 4)**

5. Brush the entire composition with two thin coats of thin-bodied white glue or decoupage medium to seal the images. Use a foam brush to apply. Let dry completely before proceeding.

6. Paint the screw-on band.

7. Apply a two-part resin coating (see the Supplies & Techniques section for instructions) to the jar and the flat lid. After the excess resin has dripped off the lid, place the metal band on the lid. It will adhere tightly. *Option:* If you decide not to add a resin coating, four to five coats of clear-drying water-based varnish will finish your altered jar.

8. Glue the accent pieces to the jar. Decorate the screw-on band. **(photo 5, photo 6)** ❑

Photo 2 – Smoothing the paper on the jar.

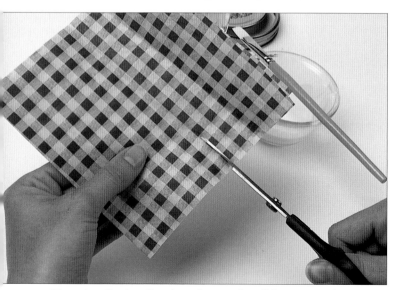

Photo 1 – Cutting slits along the top edge of the paper with scissors.

Photo 3 – Adhering images to the jar with decoupage medium.

Photo 4 – Making a collage to decorate the lid.

Photo 5 – Applying glue to the painted screw-on band.

Photo 6 – Securing the rick-rack trim with glue.

Retro 50s Jar

Pictured on page 79

SUPPLIES FOR RETRO 50S JAR

- Wide-mouth canning jar with screw-on band and metal lid
- Background paper – Red checked tissue
- Other papers – Black, white and red decorative papers, stickers to match theme (Round letter stickers add a different shape.)
- Decoupage medium
- Foam brush
- Resin coating
- Red and black buttons
- White rick-rack trim
- Red acrylic metal paint (for the lid band)
- Glue gun and clear glue sticks to glue the rick-rack trim and buttons

MEMORIES OF TUSCANY
decoupaged altered art collage jar

The background paper for this jar looks like an ancient wall, and I used the same paper to cover the flat lid. Images of angels and a cutout Tuscan landscape form the collage. To decorate the lid, I tinted a grapes charm with paint pens and placed it on the wet resin coating. The trim around the lid was glued on with a glue gun.

JAR TYPE

Wide-mouth canning jar with screw-on band and metal lid

SUPPLIES

Background paper – Tan decorative paper with cracks and swirls

Other papers – Fine art stickers, matching labels, decoupage images

White glue or decoupage medium

Embellishments and accents – Grapes charm (tinted with paint pens), 12" tan looped chenille trim, off-white piping, tan acrylic metal paint

Two-part resin coating and coating supplies

Glue gun and clear glue stick

DECORATION

Create a collage on the sides of the jar and decorate the lid, following the Basic Instructions for Altered Art Collage Jars. Use the photo as a guide. ❏

GARDEN LOVE
decoupaged altered art collage jar

The background paper for this jar is garden theme wrapping paper. Stickers, labels and cut out prints were used to create the collage. I painted the metal band with cream-colored acrylic metal paint and dry brushed it with dark brown paint for an antique look. The flat metal lid was covered with the background paper and accented with a sticker.

JAR TYPE

Wide-mouth canning jar with screw on band and metal lid.

SUPPLIES

Background paper – Garden theme gift wrap

Other papers – Flower stickers, matching labels, decoupage images Embellishments and accents – 12" moss green ribbon, green raffia, garden charms and buttons

White glue or decoupage medium

Two-part resin and coating supplies

DECORATION

Create a collage on the sides of the jar and decorate the lid, following the Basic Instructions for Altered Art Collage Jars. Use the photo as a guide.

After resin coating on the jar and lid was fully cured, I tied green raffia and moss green ribbon around the neck. Garden charms were tied on the ends of the ribbon and a garden theme button was glued at the middle of the raffia knot. ❑

EUROPEAN VACATION
decoupaged altered art collage jar

The background paper is a text weight decorative paper
with maps and vintage postcards. Stickers, labels, and
cutout images were used to create the collage.

JAR TYPE

Wide-mouth canning jar with screw on band and
metal lid

SUPPLIES

Background paper – Decorative paper with maps
and postcards

Other papers – Travel theme stickers, labels, and
decoupage images

Embellishments and accents – 20" moss green
satin ribbon, 12" thin purple ribbon, photo
frame charm, beaded tassel with travel-theme
charms, acrylic enamel paint (for lid band)

White glue or decoupage medium

Two-part resin and coating supplies

DECORATION

Create a collage on the sides of the jar and decorate
the lid, following the Basic Instructions for Altered
Art Collage Jars. Use the photo as a guide.

After the jar and lid were fully cured, satin
ribbon was tied around the neck and used to hold
a hanging photo charm. Thin purple ribbon tied
around the jar neck holds beaded tassels with
metal charms at the ends. ❑

ASIAN CANDLE HOLDER
decoupaged altered art collage jar

Use this candle holder jar as a centerpiece when you're serving Chinese or Japanese food. The background paper is rice paper with Chinese characters. Stickers, labels and cutout prints were used to create the collage. A black gros-grain ribbon was glued around the metal band and the votive candle placed inside to hold a jade colored candle.

JAR TYPE

Standard-mouth canning jar with screw on band and glass votive candle holder

SUPPLIES

Background paper – Rice paper with Chinese characters

Other papers – Asian-theme stickers, matching labels, decoupage images

Embellishments and accents – 20" celadon ribbon, 12" black grosgrain ribbon, 3 Chinese coins, tassel with coin and ivory-look bead

Two-part resin and coating supplies

White glue or decoupage medium

Jade green votive candle

DECORATION

Create a collage on the sides of the jar and decorate the screw-on band, following the Basic Instructions for Altered Art Jars. Use the photo as a guide.

After the resin coating on the jar is fully cured, place the lid on top. Tie a piece of ribbon around the jar neck and trim the tails so a short tail points up and a longer tail points down. Antique Chinese coins were glued on the jar at the ribbon knot. A bead and coin tassel hangs down over the ribbon. ❏

ANTIQUE CANISTERS
decoupaged altered art jars

These charming three canisters have vintage labels and a white crackle finish reminiscent of antique pottery. Use a clear varnish crackle, not a paint crackle that is used with acrylic paints to give a weathered painted look.
If you can't locate vintage labels, you can use decoupage paper with printed antique labels or images from a copyright-free book that includes colored vintage labels.

JAR TYPE

3 wide-mouthed canning jars with metal screw bands and metal lids

SUPPLIES FOR PAINTING & DECOUPAGE

Acrylic enamel paint – Antique white

Acrylic craft paint – White

Paint brushes – 1" flat, 1" sponge brush

Decoupage medium

Fine crackle paint kit

Acrylic paint for metal – Antique white

plus Basic painting supplies

OTHER SUPPLIES

Antique label stickers

Silicon-based glue for metal

Garden jute cord – 14" per jar

Large button – 1 per jar

JAR DECORATION

1. Basecoat the jar with antique white acrylic enamel. Let dry completely.

2. Glue the labels on the jars with decoupage medium, overlapping the images slightly, if needed, depending on the size. Reserve a label that will indicate the contents of the jar. *Option:* Use adhesive-backed stickers.

3. Brush the labels with one coat of decoupage medium. Let dry.

4. Following the instructions on the fine crackle paint kit, create a crackle finish over the labels.

5. To accentuate the crackles, antique the jars with a wash of thinned white acrylic craft paint.

6. Add the reserved labels to the fronts of the jars to indicate the contents.

LID DECORATION

1. Glue the metal lid in the band with silicone-based glue.

2. Paint the lid with acrylic paint for metal. Let dry.

EMBELLISHMENTS

1. Tie a piece of jute around the neck of each jar.

2. Glue a large, colorful button at the center of each lid. ❑

FABRIC & LACE
decoupaged jars

These three jars were covered with fabric in rose, cream, and green hues. Cotton fabrics work best. To give your fabrics a vintage, faded look, follow the directions that follow. The jars were accented with lace and lace appliques and buttons. If you are a decorative painter, you could paint roses or other motifs on the fabric after it's applied to the jar.

JAR TYPE

Canning jars with metal bands and flat lids

SUPPLIES

Cotton fabric – Prints and polka dots in rose, creams, and muted green

Cotton lace and cotton lace appliques

Polyester batting

Buttons

Rotary cutter, ruler, and cutting mat

Decoupage medium

1" flat brush

Scissors

Acrylic paint for metal – cream

Glue gun and clear glue stick

JAR DECORATION

To cover one jar

1. Use a rotary fabric cutter, ruler, and cutting mat to cut the fabric into strips 1" wide and 8" long. You will need 14 strips to cover a quart-size jar.

2. Brush decoupage medium or thin-bodied white glue on the jar.

3. Place seven fabric strips on the wet medium or glue, placing them about 3/4" apart.

4. Glue the remaining seven strips between the first strips, overlapping them so no glass shows.

5. Cover the entire surface with a thin coat of glue.

6. Cut a 3" diameter fabric circle. Glue the circle to the bottom of the jar to cover the ends of the fabric strips. Coat this end piece with a thin layer of glue. Let dry.

7. Glue pieces of lace, lace appliques, and/or fabric motifs on the jar with white glue. Let dry.

8. Brush a thin coat of glue over the lace and trim.

LID DECORATION

1. Paint the metal rings with cream metal paint.

2. Cut circles of thin polyester batting and glue to the metal lids to create soft, puffy tops.

3. Cut a 4-1/2" diameter circle of coordinating fabric. Place on the batting. Turn the edges of the fabric over the lid and glue under the lid, using a glue gun. Glue the metal lid in the band. Let dry.

4. Finish the inside of the jar lid by covering a second metal lid with fabric and gluing onto the bottom of the lid.

EMBELLISHMENTS

For each jar

1. Tear a strip of fabric and glue around the neck of the jar.

2. Accent with a button or buttons, using the photos as guides. ❑

Instructions for Vintage-look Fabric begin on page 90.

Original
fabric

Reverse
(wrong)
side

Faded with
Bleach

Tea Dyed

VINTAGE-LOOK FABRIC

Here are three methods for creating vintage-look fabrics. Use 100% cotton fabric for best results.

- **Use the fabric wrong side up.** Often, the back side of a fabric looks like a faded version of the front.

- **Fade the fabric.** Dampen the fabric with water. Fill a sink with water and add 1/2 cup chlorine bleach. Place the damp fabric in the sink and watch it fade. When the look pleases you, rinse the fabric well in clear water. TIP: The fabric looks darker when wet than it will when it dries.

- **Dye the fabric with tea.** In a glass bowl, pour boiling water over six bags of black (e.g., orange pekoe) tea. Let the tea steep for 10 minutes. Remove the teabags. Add a splash of white vinegar, then add the fabric. Let the fabric soak for a few minutes until it has changed to a nice sepia tone. Rinse the fabric well under clear water. TIP: The fabric looks darker wet than it will when it dries.

See page 88 for instructions

TRIBAL MONEY
molded polymer clay jars

This set of jar banks is very easy to make. I used polymer clay push molds created by clay artist Maureen Carlson that include matching accent words. I substituted polymer clay lids for the metal flat ones so I could cut a narrow opening for making deposits.
The jars are embellished with beads strung on wire. You can make beads from polymer clay using molds or forming them by hand.

JAR TYPE
Pint-size canning jars with metal bands

POLYMER CLAY SUPPLIES

Polymer clay – Light brown, dark brown, translucent, terra cotta, red, orange

Rubber stamps – Crackle texture, alphabet

Polymer clay molds – Tribal masks, sun

Rough textured rock

plus Basic polymer clay supplies

PAINTING SUPPLIES

Acrylic enamel paints – Avocado green, brick red, ochre

Acrylic craft paint – Brown

Acrylic paint for metal – Brick red

1" flat brush

Optional: Acrylic craft paints in bright colors, for accents

OTHER SUPPLIES

White glue

Silicone-based glue

Gold seed and bugle beads

Assorted beads

20 gauge copper, brass, or silver wire

Roundnose pliers

Wire cutters

JAR DECORATION

1. Basecoat the jars with acrylic enamel paint. Let dry.
2. Roll a thin sheet of light brown polymer clay. Tear the edges to create a 3" x 4" irregular panel. Brush white glue over the back of the clay panel and place on the front of the jar. Let the glue dry for a few minutes, then texture the panel with a crackle rubber stamp. *Option:* Use a rough textured rock.
3. Press translucent, terra cotta, dark brown, red, or orange clay into the polymer clay molds to make

the masks and letters for the words. Position them on the clay panels.

4. To add a sparkle, press seed beads and bugle beads in the clay to decorate the images.

5. Bake the jars in your home oven, carefully following the manufacturer's instructions. Let cool completely.

6. Bring out the details by applying a wash of thinned brown acrylic paint. Wipe away the excess paint immediately. *Option:* Accent some of the raised lettering with bright paint colors, using a small paint brush.

LID DECORATION

1. Roll a thin sheet of light brown polymer clay. Use the metal ring to cut a circle from the clay. Use a rough textured rock to add texture to the surface and the rubber stamp alphabet to impress words into the clay. (Mine are labeled "TRIP FUND," "SWEAR JAR," and "SPARE CHANGE.")

continued on page 95

93

HOBBIT HOUSE CANDLE
molded polymer clay jar

This jar is covered with a thin layer of polymer clay with a window cut for the lighted candle to shine through. Baking in your home oven cures the clay, and a wash of thin brown paint brings out the details. I used a cobblestone texture sheet for the "walls," but you could substitute a rough stone to create a stucco-like texture.
Use this jar as an accent in a large potted plant or in the garden.

JAR TYPE

Wide-mouth, small canning jar

SUPPLIES

Polymer clay – Transparent, light brown, medium brown, dark brown

Cobblestone texture sheet

Polymer clay push mold – Flowers and leaves

Acrylic craft paint – Brown

White craft glue

Craft knife

Toothpick

Tea light candle

Brown aquarium gravel

plus Basic polymer clay supplies

JAR DECORATION

1. Roll out a thin sheet of transparent polymer clay, using a roller or a pasta machine.
2. Add the cobblestone texture with a texture sheet. Trim the sheet to 3" x 12".
3. Coat the jar with a thin layer of white craft glue. (This helps the clay stick to the slick glass surface.) Wrap the clay around the jar and trim where it joins so it matches perfectly.
4. Immediately cut a window 2-1/2" x 1/2" from the clay and remove. Clean the glue from the window glass.
5. Make the window frame by marbling dark brown and light brown polymer clays. Roll out and cut 1/4" strips. Trim and place the strips to frame the window. Use a toothpick to mimic nail holes at the ends of the window frame pieces.
6. To make the thatched roof, roll out medium brown clay and trim to a 1-1/2" x 12" strip. Using a craft knife, make cuts along the strip by pouncing the knife on the clay to fringe it. Brush a thin layer of glue to the top of the jar. Pick up the fringed strip carefully and wrap around the top of the jar.
7. Make two thin coils of dark brown clay. Wrap them around the roof at the top and around the middle. Use the photo as a guide for placement.
8. Add tiny pieces of medium brown clay over the top of the lower dark brown coil.
9. Use a polymer clay push mold to make flowers and greenery. Press them on the side of the little house.
10. Bake the house in your home oven, carefully following the manufacturer's instructions. Let cool completely.
11. Bring out the details by applying a wash of thinned brown acrylic paint over the surface. Wipe away the excess paint immediately.

EMBELLISHMENTS

1. Cover the "floor" inside with brown aquarium gravel.
2. Place a tea light inside. ❑

TRIBAL MONEY
continued from page 93

2. Add a small face accent or cut a slit for inserting money.
3. Bake the clay circles on a ceramic tile in your home oven, carefully following the manufacturer's instructions. Let cool completely.
4. Bring out the details by applying a wash of thinned brown acrylic paint. Wipe away the excess paint immediately.
5. Paint the jar rings with acrylic paint for metal. Let dry.
6. Glue the circle into the jar ring.

EMBELLISHMENTS

1. Make the beaded accents (they look like long earrings) by cutting a 3" piece of 22-gauge wire. Coil one end and string on a few beads. Make a small loop at the top with roundnose pliers. (You'll run the base wire through this top loop.)
2. For each jar, string beads and accents on a 12" length of 20 gauge wire.
3. Wrap the strung beads around the necks of the jars. ❑

MAKING EMBELLISHED LIDS
critter lids

The decorated critter lids on the following pages were designed for jars that hold favorite layered mixes or treats. Paint pens were used for simple lettering on the outside of the jars. The features – eyes, carrot nose, ears, horns, noses, beaks, tongues, and coal pieces for the snowman's smile – were all made with polymer clay. Embellished lids are surprisingly easy to make and are a perfect project for older children to help with. All the supplies are inexpensive and easy to find.

JAR TYPE

Quart canning jar with a standard mouth and plastic storage lid or metal screw-on band and flat lid

BASIC SUPPLIES

Plastic foam balls, 3" and 1"

Texture paint – white

Features made from polymer clay

Polymer clay varnish – gloss

Acrylic craft paints

Clay facial parts for critter lids

BASIC TOOLS

Serrated knife

Toothpicks

Wooden skewer

Palette knife

Glue gun and clear glue stick

Forming an animal nose of clay

BASIC INSTRUCTIONS FOR EMBELLISHED LIDS

1. *For the head,* cut one-third away from a 3" foam ball, using a serrated knife.
   To make the cheeks, cut a 1" foam ball in half.
   For the muzzle, cut away one-third from a 1" foam ball and mold the foam with your fingernail.

2. Position the cheeks and/or muzzle on the head. Break a toothpick and use the pieces to attach the smaller foam pieces firmly in place.

3. Spear the head from the bottom with a wooden skewer. (This gives you a handle while you work.) Use a palette knife to apply texture paint over the curved part of the foam ball. You can smooth out the paint (as was done on the cow and snowman) or dab to create a furry texture (as was done on the chick, dog, bunny, and cat). Place the textured head in a jar and allow to dry thoroughly.

4. While the texture paint is drying, make the features with polymer clay. Form the pieces on a ceramic tile and bake in your home oven according to the manufacturer's instructions. Let cool.

5. Brush the polymer clay feature pieces with high gloss polymer clay varnish. Let dry.

6. Use acrylic craft paints to paint the dry, textured head. Use light pink paint to add blush to the cheeks.

7. Glue on the polymer clay features with a glue gun. You can push the ears right into the foam ball for extra stability.

8. Paint the lid and let dry. Glue head on lid. ❏

Pictured left: Snowman & Smiles Embellished Lid.
Instructions are on page 100.

CUTE CRITTERS
embellished lids

Cat Lid

LID DECORATION

See the Basic Instructions at the beginning of this section.
Face – 3" plastic foam ball for head, one 1" foam ball for cheeks
Acrylic craft paint – Orange for head, pink for cheeks
Polymer clay features – Eyes, green nose, orange ears, pink tongue
Embellishments – Green felt strip, 1/2" x 10", with orange - dimensional paint footprints

JAR DECORATION

"PURRR...MEOW" or "KITTY TREATS" written on front of jar with a green paint pen

CONTENTS IDEAS

Cat treats; catnip; licorice sticks ❏

Chicken Lid

LID DECORATION

See the Basic Instructions at the beginning of this section.
Face – 3" foam ball for head, one 1" foam ball for cheeks
Acrylic craft paint – Bright yellow, pink cheeks
Polymer clay features – Eyes, orange beak
Embellishments – Yellow feathers pushed in the top of head; yellow felt strip collar, 1/2" x 10", with dimensional painted stars

JAR DECORATION

"TWEET, TWEET, CHIRP, CHIRP, PEEP, PEEP" written around jar with black paint pen

CONTENTS IDEAS

Chicken noodle soup mix; birdseed; candy corn; popcorn kernels ❏

Dog Lid

LID DECORATION

See the Basic Instructions at the beginning of this section.
Face – 3" foam ball for head, one 1" foam ball for cheeks
Acrylic craft paint – Purple with a green spot, pink cheeks
Polymer clay features – Eyes, purple nose, purple ears, pink tongue
Embellishments – Green felt strip collar, 1/2" x 10", with mini orange buttons and a metal dog tag

JAR DECORATION

"WOOF...RUFF...BARK" or "FIDO'S FAVORITES" written on front of jar with a purple paint pen

CONTENTS IDEAS

Homemade doggy treats; dog chews; rawhide bones; doggy breath mints; lollipops ❏

Snowman & Smiles Lid
Pictured on page 97

LID DECORATION

See the Basic Instructions at the beginning of this section.

Face – 3" plastic foam ball for head, one 1" foam ball for cheeks

Paints – Sparkle white texture paint and pink paint on cheeks; snowflake sequins were placed in the wet paint on the top of the snowman's head.

Polymer clay features – Eyes, orange carrot nose, dark blue coal pieces

Embellishments – Green felt strip for scarf, 1/2" x 20", with a large red button accent; earmuffs made with a green glitter stem and two glitter pom-poms

JAR DECORATION

White snowflakes and instructions for using the hot cocoa mix inside.

CONTENTS IDEAS

Hot cocoa mix and mini marshmallows; candy canes ❑

Bunny Lid

LID DECORATION

See the Basic Instructions at the beginning of this section.

Face – 3" plastic foam ball for head, one 1" foam ball for cheeks, one 1" foam ball for muzzle

Acrylic craft paint – Pale pink, pink cheeks

Polymer clay features – Eyes, pink nose, pink and purple ears, pink tongue

Embellishments – Glitter pink pom-pom tail; pink felt strip collar, 1/2" x 10", with a purple acrylic gem heart accent

JAR DECORATION

"SOME-BUNNY LOVES YOU!" written on front of jar with a pink paint pen

CONTENTS IDEAS

Jelly beans; gumdrops; marshmallows; chocolate eggs; chocolate brownie mix ❑

Cow Lid

LID DECORATION

See the Basic Instructions at the beginning of this section.

Face – 3" plastic foam ball for head, one 1" foam ball for muzzle

Acrylic craft paints – White with purple spots, pink cheeks

Polymer clay features – Eyes, purple nose, purple ears, yellow horns

Embellishments – Purple felt strip collar, 1/2" x 10", with a purple acrylic gem heart accent

JAR DECORATION

"MOOOO..." or "UDDERLY DELICIOUS" written on front of jar with a white paint pen

CONTENTS IDEAS

Mocha coffee mix, flavored coffee, red licorice twists; chocolate-covered caramel candies ❑

FRUIT & FLOWER SEWING KITS

decorative lids

These recycled baby food jars have pincushion tops and mini sewing kits inside. They're a perfect bazaar item or office gift. The decorative pins for the pincushion tops are simply beads threaded on straight pins and glued with strong silicone-based jewelry glue. TIP: Use a toothpick to add a tiny drop of glue between the bead and the head of the pin.

JAR TYPE

Recycled baby food jar and lid

BASIC SUPPLIES

2" plastic foam ball – 1 per jar

Serrated knife

Polyester batting

Fabric or felt

Glue gun and clear glue stick

Spray paint

Sheer ribbon – 12" per jar

Rick-rack or trim (to cover rim of lid)

Novelty buttons

Sewing kit – felt, needles, safety pins, thimble

Decorative-tip straight pins

Paint pen

BASIC INSTRUCTIONS

1. Cut away one-third of the plastic foam ball, using a serrated knife.

2. Cover the ball with a thin layer of polyester batting and a 6" piece of fabric or felt. Stretch the fabric around the ball and glue the excess fabric on the bottom with a glue gun.

3. Hot glue the ball on the top of the lid, using a fair amount of glue. Hold firmly in place until cool and secure.

4. Glue trim around the rim of the lid.

5. Spray inside the jar with two coats of spray paint. Let dry completely. (The paint won't dry if the lids are put back on too soon.)

6. Tie a sheer ribbon around the neck of the jar. Accent with novelty buttons.

7. Write a message on the jar with a paint pen.

8. Fill the jar with a mini sewing kit: A 2" x 5" strip of felt cut with pinking shears holds a few needles and some safety pins, a thimble, and a small spool of thread.

9. Stick a few decorative pins in the pincushion. ❑

Watermelon Jar

Fabric for pincushion: Red fabric or felt

Lid accents: Black-headed pins glued into the pincushion

Trim around lid: Green satin ribbon, white rick-rack

Bow: Bright green sheer ribbon

Decorative pins for cushion: Red glass beads and green spacer beads threaded on black-headed pins

Spray paint for jar: Dark green ❑

Flower Jar

Fabric for pincushion: Yellow fleece or felt

Lid accents: White-headed pins glued into the pincushion; silk pink petals and green leaves are glued between the covered foam ball and the jar lid (See the photos.)

Trim around lid: Yellow grosgrain ribbon

Bow: Bright pink sheer ribbon

Decorative pins for cushion: Bee pins, made by looping a small piece of cream silk ribbon on a black-headed pin, then adding a gold diamond-shaped bead and a gold seed bead

Spray paint for jar: White ❏

Strawberry Jar

Fabric for pincushion: Red fabric or felt

Lid accents: White-headed pins glued into the pincushion

Trim around lid: Green jumbo rickrack and green satin ribbon

Bow and accent: Pale green sheer ribbon bow and a strawberry button

Decorative pins for cushion: Mini plastic flower and leaf beads threaded on a pink-headed pin to create strawberry blossom pins

Spray paint for jar: Pale green ❏

Blueberry Jar

Fabric for pincushion: Blue felt

Lid accents: Starburst gold sequin with a gold-headed pin at the center of the pincushion

Trim around lid: Green grosgrain ribbon

Bow and accent: Blue sheer ribbon bow and novelty basket button with blue beads and silk leaves

Decorative pins for cushion: Blue glass beads and gold seed beads threaded on blue-headed pins

Spray paint for jar: Dark green ❏

Supplies for the Flower Jar

Photo 1 – Gluing the fabric around the cut plastic foam ball.

Photo 2 – Arranging silk flower petals and leaves on the jar lid.

Photo 3 – Placing the fabric-covered pincushion over the flower petals.

BUTTON COLLECTION
jar with resin-coated lid

The lid on this jar has been coated with two-part resin. Items coated with resin take on an amazing new look. The tops are waterproof and can be wiped with a damp cloth when dusty. Fill the jar with vintage buttons and thread on wooden spools. The following pages show a variety of jars that have lids coated with two part resin.

JAR TYPE

Small, wide-mouth canning jar (I used an old canning jar with a glass lid, but a newer jar would also work nicely.)

SUPPLIES

Acrylic paint for metal – Cream

Silicone-based glue

Mother-of-pearl buttons and pearls

Two-part resin and basic coating supplies

Decorative trim – 12" cream

Glue gun and glue stick

LID DECORATION

1. Paint the metal band with a cream acrylic metal paint. Let dry.

2. Glue the lid into the metal ring with silicone-based glue.

3. Arrange the white and mother-of-pearl buttons on the lid. Glue in place with silicone-based glue. Add a few pearls for accents.

4. Following the instructions in the Supplies & Techniques section for two-part resin coating, coat the top and sides of the lid. Let the resin cure. Sand off any drips from the bottom of the lid.

5. Glue cream trim around the lid. ❑

VEGETABLE HARVEST
jar with resin-coated lid

This lid is the perfect top for a jar containing a layered bean or vegetable soup mix. The top is waterproof and can be wiped with a damp cloth when dusty.

JAR TYPE

Quart size wide-mouth canning jar with a metal band and lid

SUPPLIES

Acrylic paint for metal – Green

Silicone-based glue

Miniature artificial vegetables

Two-part resin coating and basic coating supplies

LID DECORATION

1. Paint the metal band and lid with green acrylic metal paint. Let dry.

2. Glue the lid into the metal ring with silicone-based glue.

3. Arrange the mini vegetables on the lid and glue in place with silicone-based glue.

4. Following the instructions in the Supplies & Techniques section for two-part resin coating, coat the top and sides of the lid. Let the resin cure. Sand off any drips from the bottom of the lid. ❏

MOSAIC
jar with resin-coated lid

Both the sides of the jar and the jar lid were coated with the resin coating to make the transparent plastic mosaic pieces look like part of the jar. If you're unable to find small plastic mosaic pieces, use glass mosaic pieces or pieces of broken pottery. Fill the jar with bath salts. The top is waterproof and can be wiped with a damp cloth when dusty.

JAR TYPE

Small wide-mouth canning jar (I used an old canning jar with a glass lid.)

SUPPLIES

Acrylic paint for metal – Purple

Silicone-based glue

Plastic mosaic pieces – blue, pink, purple

Two-part resin coating and basic coating supplies

LID DECORATION

1. Paint the metal band with purple paint. Let dry.

2. Glue the lid into the metal ring with silicone-based glue.

3. Arrange the mosaic pieces on the lid and around the lower part of the jar.

4. Following the instructions in the Supplies & Techniques section for two-part resin coating, coat the sides of the jar and pour resin into the well on top of the lid. Let the resin cure. Sand off any drips from the bottom of the jar. ❏

COUNTRY HARVEST
embellished jar

A little embellishment can make a plain jar a delightful, decorative accent. This apple-and-spice-studded jar is a perfect accent for a country kitchen. The jar is filled with an attractive layered potpourri and decorated with fabric yo-yos and cinnamon sticks.

MAKING LAYERED POTPOURRI

A glass jar is an attractive way to display these fragrant collections of dried botanicals and spices – simply layer them in the jar, pressing down each layer, and add fragrance to the top. Remove the lid to release the fragrance, or put 1/4 cup in a saucepan with water and place on low heat for a simmering potpourri. Refresh by adding additional fragrance oils as needed.

Country Apple Potpourri Recipe

1 cup dried apple slices	1/2 cup bay leaves
1/2 cup cinnamon pieces	1 vanilla bean, chopped
1/4 cup whole rose hips	1 tablespoon whole cloves
1/4 cup allspice berries	1 tablespoon whole cardamom
1/4 cup star anise	Fragrance oils – 10 drops green apple, 8 drops cinnamon

JAR TYPE

Old fashioned wire-bail type canning jar

SUPPLIES

Cotton fabric

Needle and strong buttonhole tread

Glue gun and clear glue sticks

1" pieces of cinnamon sticks

Novelty buttons – Country hearts, stars

Wire cutters (to remove shanks from buttons)

Natural raffia

Country apple simmering potpourri

EMBELLISHMENTS

1. To make a 1-1/2" diameter yo-yo, cut a 3" circle from cotton fabric.

2. Thread a needle with strong buttonhole thread that matches your fabric and sew a running stitch all around the circle 1/8" from the edge. Pull the thread to gather the stitches and flatten the piece. *Option:* Purchase ready-made yo-yos at fabric and craft stores.

3. Using a glue gun, attach fabric yo-yos around the top of the jar. Make sure you can still easily open and close the jar.

4. Glue a row of cinnamon stick pieces around the jar.

5. Remove the shanks from the buttons with wire cutters. Glue a button at the center of each yo-yo.

6. Tie natural raffia around the cinnamon sticks and knot. Glue a yo-yo over the knot.

7. Fill the jar with country apple simmering potpourri. (Recipe above.) ❏

MEMORY JARS

Why not make memory pages to put in a jar? Designed with basic scrapbooking supplies, the jar can be used as a candle holder or topped off with a fancy lid and filled with memorabilia. Start with photographs you'd like to use, and from there develop the theme for your jar. Many different coordinated theme packages are available for easy page construction at stores that sell scrapbooking supplies.

BASIC SUPPLIES

Quart-size canning jar

Photographs or photocopies of photographs

Background paper – 12" x 12"

Stickers and accents to match your theme

Scrapbook adhesives

Tissue paper

Ribbons, fibers, and embellishments to match your theme

Pictured right: Placing a rolled memory page in a jar.

BASIC INSTRUCTIONS FOR MEMORY JARS

1. Cut a piece of the background paper 5" x 12". This paper is your page – add cropped and framed photos, stickers, handwriting, and other accents. Keep the focal point of the design, usually a photograph, in the center of the paper so it is center to the composition.

2. When you are satisfied with the page design and have secured all the pieces, roll the page carefully and drop into the jar.

3. Place crumpled tissue paper in the jar to press the decorated paper against the inside of the jar.

4. Decorate the jar with ribbon, fibers, buttons, and other scrapbooking embellishments. ❏

ROMANCE
memory jar

Wedding pictures and the theme of love was used for this candle holder. It would make a great anniversary gift or Valentine's Day table decoration. The embellishments were part of a scrapbooking page package.

JAR TYPE

Standard quart-size canning jar

EMBELLISHMENTS

• Clear acrylic letters, hearts, paper, accent and border stickers (from a package designed by Heidi Grace)
• Three-dimensional hearts were glued on the outside of the jar
• Funky fibers are tied around the jar and accented at the knot with more coordinating acrylic pieces

TOP

A red glass votive candle holder is accented with clear acrylic letters ("LOVE"). A red candle is ready to light up. ❑

VACATION MEMORIES
memory jar

Photographs from a vacation at the beach were chosen for this jar that holds shells and other memorabilia. To make this jar, see the Basic Instructions for Memory Jars at the beginning of this section.

Supplies for Vacation Memories Jar

JAR TYPE
Wide-mouth quart size canning jar with metal band and lid

EMBELLISHMENTS
- Sand-colored paper and blue vellum create the backgrounds for oval-cropped photographs.
- Beach stickers accent the inside page.
- Sea theme novelty buttons (with shanks removed) are glued to the outside of the jar.
- Natural raffia and white netting are tied around the neck of the jar.

LID DECORATION
1. Glue the lid into the metal ring with clear silicone-based glue.

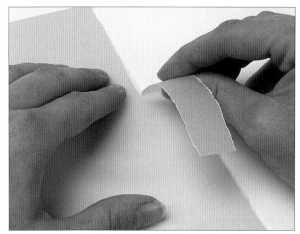
Tearing strips of vellum to decorate the background paper.

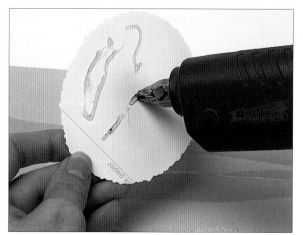
Applying glue to the back of an oval-cropped photo.

2. Paint the lid with a heavy coat of white metal paint and immediately sprinkle with white crushed coral. Let dry.

3. Arrange the shells, dried starfish, and clear glass marbles on the lid. Use the silicone-based glue to adhere them.

4. Following the instructions for the two-part resin coating in the Supplies & Techniques section, coat the top and sides of the lid. Allow the excess to drip off the sides. Let the resin cure, then sand off any drips from the bottom of the lid. ❑

BABY
MEMORIES
memory jar

A baby picture was chosen and the baby theme was used for this candle holder. Use this candle holder for a first birthday party or for a baby shower decoration. To make this jar, see the Basic Instructions for Memory Jars at the beginning of this section.

JAR TYPE

Standard quart-size canning jar

EMBELLISHMENTS

- Pastel papers and colorful stickers decorate the inside page.
- Pastel fibers, buttons, and novelty button charms decorate the outside of the jar.

TOP

A frosted glass votive candle holder holds a white candle. ❏

ARRANGEMENTS IN A JAR

The jars pictured on the next three pages have lamp kit tops and arranged contents with different themes. Jars are an excellent base for a candle or lamp. Glass votive holders for votive candles fit nicely in the top of quart-size canning jars, and you can buy oil lamp kits that fit canning jars at crafts stores. The kit includes a glass vial that holds lamp oil and a funnel for filling.
Wire around the necks of the jars provides a handle for carrying. Be sure to lower the handle when the lamp is lit so it won't get hot and accidentally burn someone.
When you give a lighted jar gift, **always** provide the recipient with instructions for use and remind the recipient to **never** leave a burning candle unattended.

BASIC SUPPLIES FOR ARRANGED JARS

Silk flowers or artificial fruits

Wire cutters

Lamp kit

Lamp oil and funnel

Vintage labels

Colored card paper

Tag template and cutter

Ribbon, tassels, beads to match theme

19 gauge black crafting wire

Acrylic paints for metal in colors to match contents

Pencil or chopstick

BASIC INSTRUCTIONS FOR ARRANGED JARS

1. Cut off the flower stems and remove leaves from the wire stems, using a pencil or a chopstick to arrange the objects. Fill the jar with silk flowers or artificial fruit, making the focal point of the arrangement in the middle of the jar and leaving space for the glass vial for the lamp oil at the top. Gluing isn't necessary.

2. Attach vintage labels to colored card paper and trim with a tag template. Hang from a ribbon tied around the neck of the jar. Add a tassel accented with beads.

3. Create a wire handle with 19 gauge wire, using the patterns provided as a guide for bending the wire. Attach to the jar by holding in place and wrapping a 12" piece of wire around the neck of the jar. Twist the ends tightly to hold.

4. The lamp kit comes with a silver finish. *Option:* Paint it with acrylic metal paint in a color that coordinates with your theme. ❑

Pears Lamp

JAR TYPE

Quart-size standard canning jar

JAR CONTENTS

Small plastic pears and green silk ivy

LID DECORATION

The lid was painted green, then spattered with brown to match the pears.

EMBELLISHMENTS

Vintage pear label tag is attached with gold ribbon and accented with a gold tassel and green and amber beads. ❏

Roses Lamp

JAR TYPE

Quart-size standard canning jar

JAR CONTENTS

Dusty pink silk roses and dried Queen Anne's Lace flowers

LID DECORATION

The lid was painted with ivory paint and brushed with brown paint to antique.

EMBELLISHMENTS

The vintage rose label tag is attached with pale green ribbon and accented with a dark brown tassel and pink beads. ❑

Grapes Lamp

JAR TYPE

Quart-size standard canning jar

JAR CONTENTS

Purple and amber artificial grapes and
leaves

LID DECORATION

The lid was painted with moss green
paint, then brushed with brown paint
to antique.

EMBELLISHMENTS

The vintage wine label tag is attached
with purple ribbon and accented with a
fiber tassel and purple beads. Purple
beads also were added to the wire
handle. ❏

Grapes Lamp

Roses Lamp

Pears Lamp

Patterns for
Lamp Handles
(actual size)

JARS FOR FOOD GIFTS
Making Homemade Mixes

Jars that hold food should be cleaned and sterilized before filling and should never be painted or decorated on the inside. Each mix recipe comes with preparation instructions that you can give with the jar.

GENERAL TIPS FOR PACKAGING HOMEMADE MIXES

- Layer ingredients in the jar in the order given in the recipe.

- Wipe down the sides of the jar with a clean paper towel after adding powdery ingredients, such as powdered (icing) sugar, cocoa, or flour before adding the next ingredient for a better appearance.

- Pack down all ingredients firmly. If you don't, you won't have enough space to fit in all the ingredients. (You will be surprised at how flour packs down!) Generally, a quart jar holds 6 cups of packed down ingredients; a pint jar holds 3 cups packed down ingredients. This is, however, a very general observation, as each recipe is made up of different ingredients that all pack down differently.

- If your ingredients do not come to the top of the jar, fill with crumpled plastic wrap or wax paper to prevent the ingredients from shifting and mixing.

Recipe Cards & Labels

When taking the time to create a decorated jar of layered cookie or soup mix, make sure you give the same attention to the instructions to make the mixes. A laminating machine does quick work to laminate recipe cards for practical use in the kitchen. Finish them off by punching a hole in the corner and hanging on the jar with elastic cord. If making lots of jars for gifts, gang up recipe instructions on one sheet for cost saving reproduction at the copy shop.

Storing Culinary Mixes

Cool, dry storage is best. **Never** store finished jars near a heat source, hot pipes, stove, or furnace or in direct sunlight. If you cannot guarantee cool and dry storage, it's better to store your mixes in the refrigerator.

One excellent quality of your homemade mixes is that they are preservative-free. For maximum freshness, label them with a "best before" date. Many factors determine the "best before" date, such as the type of flour (all-purpose flour has a longer shelf life than whole-wheat flour), preserving method (freshly dried herbs from your garden verses dried herbs bought from the market), and the general quality and freshness of the ingredients you use. These factors have been taken into account when suggesting these recommended best-before dates:

Dressing, dip, and seasoning blends – 6 months
Beans, dried vegetable soup blends – 3 months
Bread, muffin, and scone mixes – 2 weeks in the refrigerator
Cookie and cake mixes – 2 months; with nuts – 1 month
Coffee and tea mixes – 3 months

Even though many mixes would last much longer than the suggested times, the strength of the colors and flavors will fade. The goal is to provide foods that are both safe and of high quality. Remember *quality* is not the same as *safety*. A poor-quality food (such as stale cereal) may be safe to eat; an unsafe food may look and taste good but contain harmful bacteria.

Substitutions

- Low-fat mayonnaise can be substituted for regular mayonnaise.
- Yogurt can be substituted for sour cream.
- Decaffeinated instant coffee can be substituted for regular instant coffee.

Pictured at right: Soup in a Jar. Instructions follow on page 122.

CHICKEN NOODLE SOUP

- 1 jar **Chicken Noodle Soup Mix**
- 8 cups water
- 2 carrots, diced
- 2 stalks celery, diced
- ¼ cup minced onion
- 3 cup cooked chicken

Simmer all ingredients except the meat for about 15 minutes. Add the meat in last 5 minutes of cooking.

Love Mom

Soup in a Jar

Pictured on page 121

A puffy fabric-covered lid trimmed with heart-motif lace and a button tops off this jar of dry ingredients for making soup. I used a tag template and shape cutter to cut a large tag from card paper. The recipe directions were typed on a computer, printed, trimmed, and glued on the tag, which has a gingham novelty heart button as an accent. After reinforcing the hole in the tag with an eyelet, I used 15" of jute cord threaded through the hole to tie the tag to the jar.

JAR INGREDIENTS

Chicken Noodle Soup Mix

1 cup uncooked fine egg noodles

2 Tablespoons chicken bouillon powder

1/2 teaspoon pepper

1/4 teaspoon thyme

1/8 teaspoon celery seeds

1/8 teaspoon garlic powder

1 bay leaf

Combine and place in jar.

Brownies in a Jar

This recipe makes rich, chocolate-y brownies for an extra-sweet treat. Tie a 6" wooden or bamboo skewer to the jar so the recipient can check when the brownies are done.

I used a tag template and shape cutter to cut a tag from tan card paper. The tag was glued to decorative card paper, trimmed, and decorated with kitchen-theme stickers. A paper circle reinforces the punched hole in the tag, which is tied to the jar with 15" of jute cord. Similar stickers decorate the lid; a strip of the decorative card paper is glued around the screw-on band.

A self-adhesive label identifies the contents. Gel pens were used for labeling and greetings.

JAR INGREDIENTS

Chocolate Brownie Mix

Makes 5-1/2 cups

2 cups sugar

1 cup cocoa powder

1 cup all-purpose flour

1 cup chopped pecans

1/2 cup chocolate chips

Layer the ingredients in a quart-sized jar.

RECIPE

Chicken Noodle Soup

1 jar Chicken Noodle Soup Mix

8 cups water

2 carrots, diced

2 stalks celery, diced

1/4 cup minced onion

3 cup cooked chicken

Simmer all ingredients except the chicken for 15 minutes. Add the chicken and cook until heated thoroughly.

RECIPE

Chocolate Brownies

Makes 24

1 jar Brownie Mix

1 cup butter

4 eggs

Preheat the oven to 325 degrees F. Grease and flour a 13" x 9" pan. Using an electric mixer, cream the butter. Add the eggs one at a time, beating well after each addition. Add the brownie mix and mix by hand until smooth. Spread the mixture in the pan and bake 40 to 50 minutes or until a bamboo skewer or toothpick comes out clean.

Hot Cocoa Jar

Hot cocoa is a welcome winter treat, and this jar mirrors the season with snowflake motifs, blue fabric on the lid, and a frosty-looking tag.

To make the tag, I cut a 2" x 4" tag from heavy white vellum and used a decorative corner punch to punch a snowflake in each corner. The recipe directions were typed on a computer, printed, trimmed, and glued on the tag, which is accented with a novelty snowflake button. The hole was reinforced with an eyelet and 15" of thin white ribbon was threaded through the hole to tie the tag to the jar.

For the lid, cut a big scalloped edge on a circle of blue fabric. I placed the flat lid and screw-on band on the jar and glued the fabric to the band, then glued on a band of white rick-rack (See instructions for Fabric-Topped Lids) and more snowflake motif buttons

Jar Ingredients

Hot Cocoa Mix

Makes 5-1/2 cups

3 cups powdered milk

One 5 oz. package non-instant chocolate pudding mix

1/2 cup powdered non-dairy creamer

1/4 cup unsweetened cocoa powder

1/4 cup powdered (icing) sugar

Layer in a quart sized canning jar.

For one cup:
Stir contents of jar. Add 1 heaping tablespoon Hot Cocoa Mix to 1 cup boiling water.

Mocha au Lait Mosaic Jars

Decorative paper circles are an easy way to top recycled jar lids (like these colored plastic ones) and cover any unwanted design or text. A tag cut from the same decorative mosaic card paper and beads and ribbons in the colors of the paper create a coordinated look.

The recipe was typed on a computer, printed, trimmed, and glued to the tag. A 10" elastic cord was strung with about 20 glass beads and threaded through the eyelet-reinforced hole.

Jar Ingredients
Mocha au Lait Mix

Makes 3 cups

1-1/2 cups dry milk powder

1/2 cup instant coffee

1/3 cup brown sugar

2/3 cup mini chocolate chips

To make Cafe au Lait Mix, leave out the chocolate chips.

For one cup:
In a blender, combine 2/3 cup boiling water with 1/4 cup mix. Blend until frothy. Serve in a mug.

Cookie Gift Jar

A wide-mouth canning jar filled with home-made or fresh-from-the-bakery cookies is always a welcome gift. For this sophisticated dark brown-and-cream color scheme, a printed fabric (for the lid) was paired with a toile printed paper (for the tag). The edges of the fabric circle for the lid were cut with scissors; the top was padded and accented with a novelty button.

The 1-1/2" x 4" tag was cut from decorative paper. The top corners were trimmed with decorative corner punches and 15" of black satin cord was threaded through the hole to tie the tag to the jar.

More Recipes for Jar Gifts

Homemade Dog Biscuits

1 cup whole wheat flour

1/2 cup powdered milk

1/2 cup soy bacon bits

1 teaspoon sea salt

1/8 cup sugar

1 Tablespoon beef bouillon

1/4 cup water

1 egg

Preheat oven to 400 degrees F. Blend all ingredients in bowl and knead to make a dough. Roll out and cut with a bone-shaped cookie cutter. Bake 30 minutes. Turn oven down to 200 degrees F. and leave biscuits in oven to dry slowly until bone hard.

Mulled Cranberry Drink Mix

Makes 1-1/2 cups

10 cinnamon sticks

1/2 cup whole cloves

1/3 cup whole allspice

2 tablespoons dried orange peel

1/2 cup dried cranberries

Combiine all ingredients. Package 1/4 cup of the mix in a piece of cheesecloth and tie with kitchen twine. Fill a jar with cheesecloth packages of drink mix. Tie a 3" cinnamon stick to the top of the bag for a festive presentation.

METRIC CONVERSION CHART

Inches to Millimeters and Centimeters

Inches	MM	CM	Inches	MM	CM
1/8	3	.3	2	51	5.1
1/4	6	.6	3	76	7.6
3/8	10	1.0	4	102	10.2
1/2	13	1.3	5	127	12.7
5/8	16	1.6	6	152	15.2
3/4	19	1.9	7	178	17.8
7/8	22	2.2	8	203	20.3
1	25	2.5	9	229	22.9
1-1/4	32	3.2	10	254	25.4
1-1/2	38	3.8	11	279	27.9
1-3/4	44	4.4	12	305	30.5

Yards to Meters

Yards	Meters	Yards	Meters
1/8	.11	3	2.74
1/4	.23	4	3.66
3/8	.34	5	4.57
1/2	.46	6	5.49
5/8	.57	7	6.40
3/4	.69	8	7.32
7/8	.80	9	8.23
1	.91	10	9.14
2	1.83		

INDEX